Eyes and No Eyes
Vol. I

By
Arabella B. Buckley

With Forty-Eight Full Page Coloured
Plates and other Illustrations

NEW WEST PRESS

Ordering Information:
Special discounts are available on quantity purchases by corporations, associations, educators, and others. For details, contact the publisher at the listed address below.

U.S. trade bookstores and wholesalers: Please contact New West Press:

email: contact@nwwst.com

PREFACE.

These books are intended to interest children in country life. They are written in the simplest language, so as to be fit for each class to read aloud. But the information given in them requires explanation and illustration by the teacher. I have, in fact, tried to make each lesson the groundwork for oral teaching, in the course of which the children should be encouraged to observe, to bring in specimens, and to ask questions. Then when the chapter is read and re-read, as is the case with most school books, it will become part of the child's own knowledge.

No one can be more aware than I am how very slight these outlines arc, and how much more might have been given if space permitted. But I hope that much is suggested, and a teacher who loves nature will fill in the gaps.

The charming illustrations will enable the children to identify the animals and plants mentioned.

ARABELLA B. BUCKLEY

CONTENTS.

Book III.—Plant Life in Field and Garden.

Book IV.—Birds of the Air.

CONTENTS. vii

"EYES AND NO EYES"

First Book.

WILD LIFE IN WOODS AND FIELDS.

INTRODUCTION.

We three friends, Peter, Peggy and Paul, walk to school together every day. We all love flowers and animals, and each day we try to find something new.

Peter is a little boy. He can only just read. But he has sharp eyes. He sees most things in the hedges. Peggy's father is a gamekeeper. She knows the birds and where to find their nests. Paul comes from the farm. He is a big boy and will soon be a teacher.

We meet at the big pond under the elm trees. Then we walk along a narrow lane, across the common, through the wood, and over three fields to the village school.

In the pond we find all kinds of creatures. In the lane are beetles and mice, flowers and berries, birds' nests and wasps' nests. On the common the spiders spin their webs on the yellow gorse. In the ploughed field the lark hides her nest. In the grass field there are buttercups and daisies. In the cornfield there are poppies and cornflowers.

Paul is going to write down for us all we see and put it in a book.

LESSON I.

SPIDERS ON THE COMMON.

WHEN we cross the common on a fine summer morning we see many spiders' webs sparkling in the sun. The webs on the gorse bushes are round. They are fastened to the gorse prickles by long silk threads, and each web has spokes like a wheel. These spokes are joined together with rings of silk. There are drops of gum all over the rings. It is these drops which sparkle like diamonds, and make the web so pretty.

The spider spins a little tent in the centre of the web. In this tent she hides, till some insect flies against the gummy threads. Then she feels the web shake, and darts out to catch the fly before it breaks the threads.

We saw a little bee to-day fly right against the web on the gorse bush. Out came the spider from her tent. She bit the bee with her sharp fangs, tore off its wings, and then sat and sucked the juice out of its body.

Paul caught her, while she was busy, and showed us the two fangs with sharp points, which hang down in front of her

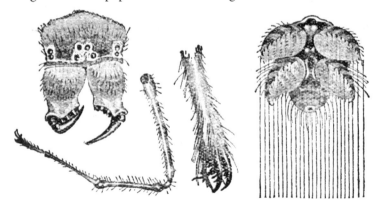

HEAD, LEG, CLAW AND SPINNERETS OF A SPIDER
MUCH MAGNIFIED.

A GARDEN SPIDER AND BLACKBERRY BRANCH.

head. Above them are her eight eyes, four large ones and four small ones. She has eight legs with such strange claws! Each one is like a comb. What do you think they are for? She uses them to guide the silk threads as she makes her web.

We turned her on her back and saw, under her body, six little pockets, out of which she pulls the silk. It comes out through tiny holes. She draws it through the combs on her legs, and so makes her web as she runs along.

Besides the webs on the gorse, there are webs all over the common close to the ground. These are not made with spokes like the round webs. The threads are mixed up like wool. For a

long time we could not find the spider. At last one day Paul said, "Here is a hole right in the middle of the web. It goes down into the ground."

This hole was lined with silk threads. Just then a bee-

HUNTING SPIDER WITH HER
EGG-BAG.

tle crawled on the web, and shook it. At once the spider darted out from the tunnel in the ground and seized the beetle. She was so quick that she had carried him down into her hole before we could catch her.

There are many spiders on the common which do not spin webs, though they hang from a thread. They spring on the flies and beetles on the ground and are called "hunting-spiders."

The mother hunting-spiders carry their eggs about with them in a round bag. Peter caught one of these as she was running along with this white ball under her body. He took the ball away and put it on the ground. When he let her go, she ran up and seized it. He took it away three times. Each time she caught it up again, and at last ran away before we could catch her.

LESSON II.

THE WOODPECKER'S NEST.

WE were lying under the shade of the trees in the wood one afternoon. All was very quiet, when suddenly we heard such a strange cry. It was like someone laughing "Yaffil, Yaffil, Yaffil." "That is the woodpecker," said Peggy. "Wait and see what he will do."

So we lay quite still under the tree. Soon the sound came nearer, and a great heavy bird, bigger than a large thrush, flew towards us. He was a beautiful bird. His wings were green, and so was his breast. He had yellow on his tail. His head was red, and he had a red streak on his throat. His beak was long and grey.

He came quite close to us, hopping along. Then he stopped, and a long shining tongue came out of his mouth, and went back so quickly that we could scarcely see it.

"He is eating ants," said Peggy. "The tip of his tongue is sticky and he draws them into his mouth."

Then he began to climb the tree so funnily. His tail is quite stiff and wiry, and he bent it against the tree, and pushed himself up, jump, jump, holding on with his sharp hooked toes. He jumped first to the right, then to the left. Then he ran round the tree and came out on the other side.

All the while he was trying the bark with his beak. Tap, tap,

tap. At last he found a soft spot. Then he tore off the bark and ate the grubs, which had made the tree rotten in that place. After this he came down the tree again.

It was so funny to see him. He came down backwards tail first, using it to steady himself. Then he spread his wings and flew slowly away.

We crept after him, and by-and-by he stopped at an old elm tree and flew round it. Then we could see no more of him.

"His nest must be in this tree," said Peter. "Give me a back, Paul, and I will soon find it."

So Paul let Peter climb on his back till he could reach the branches of the tree. Then Peter caught hold of the boughs, and crept round the trunk.

A WOODPECKER'S NEST.

"Here it is," he cried at last. "There is a small hole, just big enough for a bird to creep in. But they have made such a big hole inside the tree. I can only just reach down."

The Peter drew his hand back with the mother bird in it. Her head was not so red as the father's, and she had no red

WOODPECKERS.
OLD COCK BIRD, BELOW; YOUNG FULLY-FLEDGED BIRD, ABOVE.

whiskers. He let her fly away and then pulled out six white shining eggs.

"I can feel a number of soft chips of wood at the bottom of the hole," said he. "Shall I put the eggs back?"

"Of course," said Paul; "then the mother will fly back and sit on them, and we will come again and see the little birds when they are hatched."

So we went away. But every day, as we came from school, we turned aside to see if the little woodpeckers had come out of their shells.

At last one day we saw the old woodpeckers carrying insects into the hole. After some time we saw the young birds out on the tree. They could not fly. But they ran about the branches, and jumped so funnily with their stiff tails.

A week later we saw them flying about, and when we came again they were all gone. Peter climbed up and found the nest quite empty.

LESSON III.
SPRING FLOWERS.

WE are always glad when April comes. Then we can find many flowers on our way to school. Even in February there are snow-drops in the orchard and Peter knows where he can some-times find a primrose or violet in flower.

But we cannot get a good bunch until April. Before that the plants are busy growing their leaves.

The first bright flowers we find are the daffodils in the fields, and the anemones in the woods. We call the daffodils "Lent lilies" and we put them in the church at Easter. They have very long, narrow leaves which come straight out of the ground. Each flower hangs on its own tall stalk. It has deep yellow tube in the middle, with a crown of pale yellow leaves round it. If you dig up a daffodil plant you will find that it has a bulb like an onion. Paul says this is why it blooms so early. It stores up food in the bulb in the autumn. Then it uses this food in January to make its leaves and flowers.

DAFFODILS AND ANEMONES.

The wood-anemone is Peggy's favourite flower. It is called the "wind-flower" because it nods so prettily in the wind. Its soft pink and white flower stands high up on a long stalk, which has three feathery green leaves halfway down. When the sun shines, it is a little pink and white cup, and when the clouds gather and the rain falls, it shuts up in a tight bud, till sunshine comes again.

Peggy once bit one of the leaves of the anemone. It burnt her tongue and tasted very bitter. Then Paul told us that the plant is poisonous. This is one reason why there are so many anemones in the wood. Animals will not eat the leaves, but leave them alone to grow.

The anemone has not got a bulb. It has a thick brown stem under the ground in which it stores its food.

Before the daffodils and anemones are over, the primroses and violets cover the banks. It is pretty to watch the primrose plant on a wet morning. The leaves are not smooth. They have hills and valleys all along them. The water runs so cleverly down the valleys of the leaf. These guide it down to the roots, so that the plants can drink.

How busy, too, the bees and flies are. They settle first on one primrose then on another. We know what they find there. If you pull off the yellow crown of the primrose, and suck the end of the tube, you will taste something sweet. This is the honey that the bees come to find. And besides the honey they carry off some yellow dust from flower to flower. Paul says this is good for the flowers, as we shall learn some day.

The honey in the violets is not so easy to find. But we have found it. When a violet looks straight at you, it shows five purple leaves and a little yellow beak in the middle. But if you look behind, you will find a small long bag, like the finger of a glove. We have often pulled this off and sucked it. It is full of honey. When the bee sits on the flower, and thrusts her head into the yellow beak in the middle, she sips out the honey with her tongue from the bag or spur behind the flower.

With primroses and violets and blue-bells the bees can now find plenty of honey to fill their hives.

LESSON IV.

A FAMILY OF SQUIRRELS.

WE have a pet called Bobby, and we love him very much. He is a little squirrel, living among the beech trees of the wood.

We see him every morning leaping from branch to branch, with his long furry tail stretched out behind. Sometimes he leaps right down on to the ground and runs about picking up beech nuts.

Sometimes he sits bolt upright on a branch, with a nut or acorn in his paws. Then his tail is bent up against his back.

We have known him for two years, and when we whistle to him he comes to us. But if anything frightens him he darts away to the nearest tree. He climbs up in a moment with his sharp claws, and peeps back through the green leaves. We see his bright black eyes looking down at us.

His back is covered with a brown red fur, but under his body the fur is white. His lovely red tail is like a brush on his back. His hind legs are long. That is why he can jump so well. On his front paws one toe stands out from the others, almost like our thumb. He uses his paws like hands, when he sits up with a nut in them, and peels off the brown skin with his teeth.

Sometimes he steals birds' eggs. Then he holds the egg in his paws, cracks the top, and sucks out the yolk.

He has such funny ears! They have long tufts of hair behind them. He sometimes comes out of his hole in winter to eat, and we see that the tufts are much longer then than in summer.

But for most of the winter we never see him. He is fast asleep in a hole in a tree. We know where his hole is, for Peter

A PAIR OF SQUIRRELS.

found it once. He had seen Bobby come down one mild day to feed on his store of acorns, buried at the foot of the tree, and he watched him as he went back. Then he climbed up the tree, and in a hole in the trunk he saw Bobby's bushy tail curled round. So he knew that Bobby was snug and cosy in the hole.

Bobby has a little wife, and they always keep near each other. But she is very shy, and will not come to us. In the spring, when there are no nuts, they eat the buds of the trees.

About May they are very busy. They gather leaves, and moss, and twigs. These they weave into a nest in the fork of the tree, far from the ground. Then in June their little ones are born. Paul climbed up and saw four such lovely little squirrels, covered with soft red and white fur. They stayed in the nest for some time, though we often saw them moving about among the branches. The old squirrels took such care of them, and they stayed together all the summer. In the autumn they hid little heaps of nuts and acorns at the foot of the tree, to eat when they should awake in the mild days in winter.

Then we did not see them again. We do not know whether they all crept into one hole, or whether they each found a hole, and curled themselves up to sleep.

LESSON V.

THE SKYLARK AND HER ENEMY.

THERE are a great many larks near our home. They sing so gaily in the morning as we go to school. But they sing much earlier than that.

We wanted once to try if we could get up before the lark. So we agreed to meet at five o'clock in the morning, in the meadow where one has been singing all this year. We heard him before we got out of the lane. There he was, rising up into the air, going a little to the right, and then a little to the left, rising and singing all the time, as if he wanted to wake all the world with joy.

We watched him till he was quite a tiny speck in the sky. The he came down again. When he was only a few feet from the ground he shut his wings and dropped into the grass.

The next morning we went at four o'clock. That lark was not singing, but one in the next field was rising up as gay as a lark could be. Then our mothers said we must not get up any earlier. So we could not rise before the larks.

We caught a lark once to look at it, and then let it fly away again. It is not a gay bird. It has brown wings marked with dark streaks. Its breast and throat are a dull white, dotted with brown spots, and it has a white streak above its eye. Its feet are curious. The toes lie flat on the ground, and the hind toe has a very long claw. If you watch a lark you will see that he runs, he does not hop. Neither does he perch in the trees, and only sometimes on a low bush. He lives on the ground, except when he rises up to sing.

In the winter, as we go to school, we see large flocks of larks in the fields, looking for insects, and seeds of wheat and oats. When we come near them, they get up, a few at a time, and fly away a little further. Then they wheel round and settle down to feed.

In the winter they scarcely ever sing. It is in the spring, when they pair, that they sing so beautifully.

About March we can often find a lark's nest hidden in the

A LARK ESCAPING FROM A HAWK.

grass. They build in a rut, or a little hollow in the ground, often in the middle of the field. They line the nest with dry grass, and lay four or five eggs in it. The eggs are a dirty grey colour with brown spots on them, and they lie very snugly in the thick tufts of grass.

When the lark comes down after singing he does not drop close to the nest but a little way off. The he runs up to the nest through the grass. This is because he is afraid that the sparrow-hawk might see the nest, and pounce on the little ones.

The sparrow-hawk is the lark's great enemy. One day we were looking at lark rising up, and all at once we saw a sparrow-hawk just going to pounce upon it. The lark saw him too, and darted up faster than the hawk could soar. Then the hawk flew

THE LARK SOARING.

away a little and hovered about till the lark was tired and was obliged to come down. Then once more the hawk tried to pounce. But the lark was too clever for him. He closed his wings and dropped right down into the thick grass, and the hawk could not find him. We were glad the little lark was safe, and got back to his wife and little ones.

LESSON VI.

NUTS AND NUT-EATERS.

WE pass through a small nut-wood on our way to school. In the winter, when there are no leaves on the trees, we see the grey clusters which we call "lambs-tails" hanging on the nut-bushes, Paul says their real name is "catkins."

We often look at them to see how they grow. At first they are only like little grey buds on the branch. Then they grow larger and hang down. By degrees they become very loose, like tassels, and under the grey scales come some little bags of yellow dust.

Then in March, still before the leaves are on the trees, the wind shakes the tree and blows the yellow dust about.

By this time we find small flowers, growing near the end of the branches. You have to look well to find them. But they are very pretty. Each flower has two tiny red horns, and there are many flowers in one green cup.

We know that these red flowers grow into nuts, for we find the nuts just in that place in September. When the wind blows the yellow dust out of the lambs-tails, some of it falls on the red horns of the flowers, and this makes the nut grow.

In the autumn we look out well to see when the nuts are ripe. We want to get some before the Squirrels, and the little birds called Nuthatches, carry them all away.

Peggy is in such a hurry that she picks them sometimes before they are ripe. This is foolish, for then there is only a very small watery kernel inside. The rest of the shell is filled with white soft stuff.

Paul says this white stuff is the food which the nut uses to

THREE KINDS OF WILD NUTS, RED-TIPPED NUT-FLOWERS
AND CATKINS ON A BRANCH.

make itself large and firm. When the nuts are ripe they drop quite easily out of the brown leafy cup in which they sit.

Sometimes when we pick the nuts we find one with a little hole in the shell. Then we know that the nut is a bad one, and we shall most likely find a maggot inside.

It is so curious! Paul tells us that this maggot is a young beetle. It does not look like one. But many beetles when they are young have no legs and are only grubs.

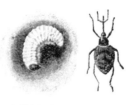

NUT WEEVIL AND GRUB.

This nut-beetle is called a Weevil. When the nut is quite young and soft, the mother weevil comes and lays an egg in it. She is a very small beetle and has a long snout. With her snout she makes a hole in the soft green nutshell, and then lays a tiny egg in the

MAGGOTY NUTS.

hole. By-and-by the egg hatches into a maggot. It grows fat by feeding on the nut. So when we gather it, the nut is half eaten, and the maggot is curled up inside.

If we had not picked the nut, the maggot would have eaten a large hole in the nutshell with its horny mouth, and then have crept out of its maggot skin as a little weevil with wings.

So the yellow dust and the red flowers make nuts. Some of these nuts we get. Some the squirrels get. Some the nuthatch gets. Some fall to the ground and grow up into young nut trees, and some the weevil grub gets, before they are ripe.

LESSON VII.

THE MOUSE AND THE SHREW.

PETER has a fine old cat. She is very clever. She rattles the handle of the front door when she wants to come in. If she comes home very late at night she jumps on the wire which runs along the garden wall. This rings a bell, and Peter comes down and lets her in.

But in one thing she is very stupid. She cannot learn that a shrew and a mouse are not the same kind of animal. We are glad when she catches the mice in the garden and in the field. For the mice eat our peas and the bulbs of our crocuses. They hide in the corn-ricks and eat the wheat and oats.

But shrews eat insects and worms and slugs, and this is good for us, because insects and slugs eat our plants.

It is so silly of Pussy, for she ought to know. When she has killed them, she does know them apart, for she eats a mouse and likes it, but she will not eat the shrew. She only kills it and leaves it lying on the path. We think she kills if because it runs away; and does not eat it because it has a bad smell.

A great many people do not know a mouse from a shrew, for they are very much alike. A shrew is not quite so large as a field-mouse, and a little larger than the dear little harvest mouse, which makes a round nest of dry grass among the corn-stalks.

We found one of these nests last summer. It was about as big as a large swan's egg, and the same shape. We peeped inside and found seven wee little harvest-mice, with red-brown fur on their backs and white fur underneath.

The shrew is more of a grey colour. But there is one way by

HARVEST MICE WITH NEST — ABOVE.
AND FIELD MOUSE — BELOW

which you can always tell a mouse from a shrew. The mouse has a short snout, and four broad white teeth in front. It uses these for gnawing roots and bulbs, and biting the ears of corn.

But the shrew has a long, thin snout, and its crown teeth are very small and pointed, so that it can kill and eat insects, worms, and snails.

Shrews and mice are both very busy in the evening. We go out sometimes to watch them when the moon is shining. The mice run along so fast out into the field and back to the hedge. Paul says they are carrying seeds and bits of roots into their hole in the bank. For they know that they will want food when they wake up in the winter, and there is none to be found. The shrews move

BARN-OWL AND SHREW.

more quietly under the hedge. They push their long snouts into the thick grass, and eat the earwigs and caterpillars.

Both the mice and the shrews are very much afraid of the Barn Owl, which comes out at night and carries them away in her sharp claws to feed her young owls.

Shrews do not store up food, for they sleep in a hole in the bank all the winter through. Then in the spring they line the hole with soft dry grass, and there the mother brings up five or six little shrews.

The mouse, too, burrows deep into the bank. She lays up a nice store of food and goes to sleep. But she often wakes and has a feed, and goes to sleep again. She brings up a great many families in a year. That is why there are so many mice.

LESSON VIII.
THE ANT-HILL.

THERE is a big ant-hill in the wood on the way to school. It is at the foot of the old oak tree, near the path, and is almost as tall as Peter. It looks like a loose heap of leaves, mixed with sticks and earth. It is broad at the bottom, and round at the top.

When we come home in the evening all is quiet on the ant-hill. We cannot see even one ant outside. It looks as if no one lived there. But when we pass in the morning, and the sun is warm and bright, we can see the ants creeping out of the cracks and running about the heap.

They are as big as a grain of barley, and have a tiny knob in the middle of their body. They have long feelers and strong jaws. They bite hard of you touch them. But they do not sting with their tails, as our house ants do.

At dinner-time we find them still more busy. They have opened many holes in the hill, and hurry to and fro. Some fetch bits of leaves and sticks, and add them to the heap. Others bring in food. One day Paul saw a number of ants pulling a dead worm to pieces. Then each ant carried a tiny bit in her jaws to the hill, and went in at a hole.

Sometimes the ants bring some little white lumps in their mouths out of the hill. Peggy's father, the gamekeeper, gives these white lumps to his birds to eat. He calls them ant-eggs. But Paul says they are not eggs. They are baby ants shut up in silk bags, and they are called "cocoons."

Real ant-eggs are much smaller. When the baby ant comes out of the egg it is blind and has no legs. It is called a grub. The nursing ants feed it with honey, and it puts a silk thread out of its mouth and spins a bag round itself.

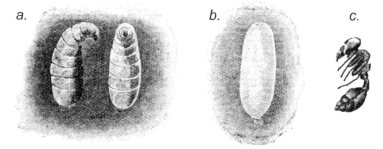

a. AN ANT-GRUB   *b.* AN ANT-COCOON   *c.* YOUNG ANT

When the bag is done, the nurses cannot feed the grub anymore. So they take care of it. They carry it up to the sunshine by day, and down below at night. Inside the bag, the grub grows into a real ant, with eyes and legs. Then the nurses help it out of its prison, and it begins to work.

One day Paul poked a hole in the ant-hill with his stick. We saw in the ground, under the leaves, a hollow place full of white cocoons. The ants were very angry. Some bit us, others picked up the cocoons in their jaws and ran away, for fear we should hurt their babies.

HILL OF THE WOOD-ANT.

When we came back in the evening the ants had mended the hill. Every hole was closed, and all the cocoons were safe inside.

One day in summer we saw a number of ants with wings, flying over the ant-hill. Paul says these are the father and mother ants. The ants without wings are the nurses and workers.

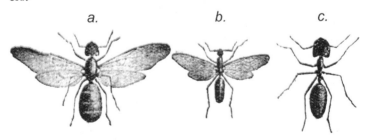

a. MOTHER ANT.   *b*. FATHER ANT.   *c*. WORKER ANT.

LESSON IX.

THE HUMBLE BEE'S NEST.

LAST March, when the days began to be warm, we saw a big Humble Bee, or Bumble Bee, as the little ones call it, buzzing along across the field.

"Look out, Peter," said Peggy; "that is a mother humble bee, who has been asleep all the winter. She must be making a nest." So Peter followed her. She flew to a bank, and went in among some tufts of grass. Peter put a large stick there and we went to see her every day.

We used to find her dragging in little pieces of moss. But we did not look in, for fear she should go away. After a fortnight Paul said we might look, and, hidden in the grass, we found a small round patch of moss lined with bees-wax. It was like a tiny saucer turned upside down. We lifted it up and found under it a few round flat pockets, some as big as a halfpenny, some not larger than a farthing. They were made of brown, sticky

A HUMBLE BEE'S NEST.

HUMBLE BEES GATHERING HONEY FROM PEA-FLOWERS.

wax, and when we opened one we found inside seven tiny eggs, as small as poppy seeds, and some little brown balls. The balls, Paul said, were made of honey, and of the yellow dust from flowers. In another pocket we found grubs which had already been hatched from eggs. These were feeding on the brown balls near them.

The mother bee was very uneasy while we were looking at her nest. She sat down quite near. We could see how big and stout she was. She was so handsome. Her brown body was covered with soft yellow hairs, with stripes of black hairs between. Her wings were broad, and shone so brightly in the sun. She did not sting us. Paul says that humble bees are very gentle. But she was afraid we would hurt the grubs, which were going to grow up into working bees. We put the cover back and waited two months. Then it was June. We were afraid the horses might tread on the nest when the hay was cut. So we went to look at it.

Oh! How big it was now. There was a large round moss roof. It was lined with wax, and was so strong that we had to cut it with a knife. The only way for the bees to get into it was by a long tunnel just under the ground. Under the roof were a number of dirty yellow silk cocoons. In these were the grubs, growing into humble bees. The cocoons were stuck together with wax. Some of them were open, for the young bees had come out. These had honey in them.

There were a great many humble bees going in and out. These had all come from eggs laid by the mother bee in two months. They were very busy bringing in honey and bee-bread for the grubs to eat. But Paul says they do not store honey, like our hive-bees. For when the cold damp weather comes, they all die, except a few mothers. These creep into holes in the trees or into a warm haystack, and sleep till the spring comes again.

About Christmas time we went to look at the nest. The roof was broken, and the cells all crushed. There was not one humble bee to be found.

LESSON X.

PETER'S CAT.

PETER'S cat is very fond of going in to the wood. We are afraid she will be killed some day. For Peggy's father shoots all the cats he finds in the wood, because they eat the rabbits and pheasants.

But Peter cannot keep her at home. As soon as it gets dusk, she slips out, and often does not come home all night. She goes in the dusk, because then all the animals are feeding. So she can catch mice and young rabbits, as well as partridges asleep on the ground, and other birds in the trees.

She is a very clever hunter. Her body is so well made for catching her prey. She is slender, but very strong. She can kill a mouse with one stroke of her paw. She can spring ever so far, and so quickly that few mice or birds can escape her.

Then she has soft pads under her feet, so that she can creep along very quietly. And she can jump down from a high wall because the soft pads keep her feet from being hurt when she reaches the ground.

We all know what sharp claws she has at the end of her toes. But when she is playing with her kitten or with Peter, her paw is so soft you would not think she could scratch. This is be-

A CAT STALKING A RABBIT.

cause she has a groove in each toe under the skin, and when she does not want her claws, she draws each one back into its own sheath.

PADS AND CLAWS ON
PUSSY'S FEET.

But when she springs on a mouse or a bird, she strikes with her paw, and as she bends her toes, out come the claws and pierce the flesh of her prey.

But how does she see the rats and mice in the night? Paul showed us that she can open the middle of her eye very wide in the dark. We took pussy near to the lamp and saw the hole or "pupil" of her eye was only a little narrow slit. Then we shut her up in dark room for some minutes, and took her outside, and looked at her eyes in the moonlight. The little slit had become a large round black hole.

The slit lets in enough light for pussy to see in the daytime, and when she goes out at night the slit stretches out into a big

round hole which lets in all the light there is, *a* from the moon or the stars.

But if it is very dark indeed, she feels her way with her whiskers. Paul says it is very *b* cruel to cut a cat's whiskers, for they are a great help to her in the dark.

Pussy has a very rough tongue. If you let her lick your hand, you will feel how differ-

CAT'S EYES
a. IN THE LIGHT
b. IN THE DARK

ent it is from your own tongue, or that of a dog. It is so rough that she can rasp the scraps of meat off a bone, after she has torn away the flesh with her long pointed front teeth.

Pussy is very clever in getting her living, and if you look at her head you will see why. For she has a good broad forehead with plenty of room inside for a large brain. We put a rabbit's head near hers the other day. It was so narrow, and had so little room for a brain we were not surprised that the cat is too cunning for him.

Who would think that Pussy, who sits and purrs with her kitten by the fire, is so fierce in the wood? But Paul says that there were once wild cats in Scotland and in the north of England, and they were as fierce as tigers. Tigers and cats are very much alike. Tigers can be loving too. We heard a tiger purr one day in a wild beast show, when she was licking her cub.

LESSON XI.

THE GREEDY STRANGER.

It was the middle of April this year when we first heard the cuckoo. We love to hear it, for it tells us that spring has come. This year we were very lucky. We saw a young cuckoo grow up in his nest.

This was how it happened.

We had heard the cuckoo for some time, cuck-oo, cuck-oo, and it seemed as if many cuckoos were singing. One day we heard such a funny noise, like kik-kik-kik. "Ah!" said Peggy, "father says that is the cry of the mother cuckoo which lays the eggs. That is why there are so many cuckoos about. They are singing to her."

"Well then," said Peter, "if she stops here, perhaps we may find one of her eggs. I do so want to see a young cuckoo."

About a week after this Peter found a titlark's nest. It was in a tuft of grass, on the bank near the wood. Two small dull-grey eggs, spotted with brown, were lying in the nest. The next day, as we went to school, there were three eggs. The next morning there were four. But as we came back from school that afternoon there were five eggs.

"The titlark cannot have laid two eggs in one day," said Peter. "I wonder if the cuckoo has brought one of her eggs here."

For we know that the cuckoo lays her eggs on the ground, and brings it in her wide beak to the nest of some other bird. We looked every day for a fortnight. The little titlark was so used to our coming, she did not even fly off the nest. She was a pretty little bird, with brown spotted wings and a yellow throat and chin.

At the end of a fortnight two little titlarks came out of their shells, and the next day two more. They opened their beaks for food, and the father titlark flew out to the field, and brought flies and caterpillars to feed them. But the mother still sat on the fifth egg.

Two day later the fifth bird came out. It had a curved beak, and bent toes with short, sharp claws. Its toes were two in front and two at the back. Titlarks have straight beaks and flat toes, three in front and one at the back.

So we knew our young cuckoo by his beak and toes.

We came next day to look. The little titlarks had quills on their wings where the feathers were growing, and their eyes were open. The cuckoo was naked and blind. But he had pushed two of the titlarks out of the nest, and they lay on the bank quite dead.

The cuckoo had grown bigger even in one day, and the old titlarks kept feeding him with insects as he sat with his beak wide open. While we were looking at him the cuckoo pushed

about in the nest and shoved another little titlark over the edge, on to the bank. We put it back in the nest and then we had to go on to school. When we came back the cuckoo sat in the nest alone. All the four little titlarks were dead on the bank. He had pushed them all out.

A CUCKOO SINGING.

The old birds did not seem to see their dead children. They were so busy feeding the big hungry stranger. They fed him for five or six weeks, even after he could come out of the nest.

It was so funny to see! The cuckoo was larger than a thrush and the titlarks not bigger than a sparrow. Yet the big bird sat on a branch with his beak open, and let these little birds carry all his food.

At last he flew away. We heard a cuckoo singing in August, when we knew the old birds were all gone. We wondered if it was our young "greedy stranger."

LESSON XII.

THE MOLE AND HIS HOME.

THERE were so many moles in the barn field last summer. We used to see mole heaps thrown up all over the field. At last Paul's father sent for the mole-catcher. He put traps in the runs and brought in many dead moles.

A mole is a curious creature. We country children call him a "wunt." He has a long, plump body, and a short, stumpy tail. His dark brown fur is like velvet, it is so soft and close. He has a long, pointed snout, very hard at the tip, and his mouth is full of strong, sharp teeth.

His feet are very curious. They have no fur on them, but are naked and pink. His front paws are like broad, flat hands with very strong claws. They turn away from his body, and look too big for such a small, soft creature.

Paul says these paws are the mole's shovels. He lives under the ground and catches worms to eat. As he goes along he makes a hole with his hard nose, and then shovels away the earth with his strong hands. In this way he makes a tunnel, and when he wants to get rid of the loose earth, he pokes it above ground with his long snout. This is how the mole-hills are made.

But the moles do not always stay under the ground. We have seen them sometimes on a warm summer's evening poking about in the hedges, looking for slugs and snails. There are more he-holes than she-holes.

We wanted so much to find a mole's home. We dug down below some of the mole-hills hoping to find one. But we only found a tunnel. The mole-catcher laughed at us for digging there. He asked us if we thought that the mole would put a heap of loose earth over his home, to tell his enemies where to find him.

At last, one day a gentleman came to Paul's father and asked him to open a mole's home for him. He wanted to see what it was like. This was just what we wanted, so we went too.

The mole-catcher took us some way across the field. At the corner near the wood we came to a large mound, under the trees, covered with grass.

MOLE EATING A WORM.

Then he began to dig away the side of the mound. By-and-bye, about the middle, he stopped and cleared away the earth very carefully with his hands. And there, just below the ground, was a big round hole covered with a roof of very hard earth. He had taken away the side, and we could see in. The hole was lined with dry grass, and in it lay four tiny moles. We filled it in again very carefully and left the baby moles safe and quiet.

We saw four holes in the sides of the nest. These led to the runs through which the old moles went in and out to feed. We are afraid they got rather filled with earth from our digging, but the mole-catcher said that they would soon be put right by the old moles.

He says that the father mole lives in another home like this all alone in winter, feeding on worms. Sometimes he comes up above the ground, and if it is very frosty weather he dies of cold. He only takes a wife in the spring.

"EYES AND NO EYES"

Second Book.

BY POND AND RIVER.

LESSON I.

A FROG'S LIFE.

CROAK, croak, croak, we hear the frogs in the month of March. They make a great deal of noise in this month, because they are just awake from their winter's sleep, at the bottom of the pond.

The mother frogs are laying their tiny dark eggs in the water. Each egg is not bigger than a grain of sand. But it has a coat of jelly, and this jelly swells and swells in the water, till it is as large as a pea, with a little black dot in the middle. The jelly lumps all cling together. You may see them in almost any pond, driven up to the side by the wind.

Soon the dark speck lengthens. A head grows at one end, and a tail at the other. The head has a mouth, but no eyes as yet. The tail has a fin all round it, and the tadpole wriggles about in its slimy bed.

In about a week it wriggles out of the jelly, and hangs by its mouth to the weeds (1). Then two curious tufts grow on each side of its head. It uses these tufts to breathe, by taking air out of the water. You can see them if you dip a glass into the pond and catch a few tadpoles.

By this time the tadpole has let go of the weed and is swimming about. A sharp beak has grown on to his mouth. He uses it to tear off pieces of weed to eat. Now he grows eyes, nose-holes and flat ears. His tufts shrivel up, and a cover grows over them (2), so that you cannot see them. They are now like the gills of a fish. He gulps water in at his mouth and sends it out through the cover. As it passes, the gills take the air out of it, and so the tadpole breathes.

Soon two small lumps appear on each side of his body, behind the cover, just where it joins his tail. They grow larger and larger, till at last two hind legs come out. These legs grow very long and strong, and he uses them to swim. Two front legs are growing as well, but you cannot see them, because they are under the cover. In a few days these peep out (3), but they are short and stumpy.

Our tadpole has now four legs and a tail. He has four toes on the front feet, and five toes on the hind feet, with a skin between the toes. So his hind legs are web-footed, and this helps him to swim.

He comes to the top of the water much more often than before, and sends a bubble of air out of his mouth. What do you think has happened? The gills under his cover have closed up, and a small air-bag has grown inside him. So he comes up to breathe in the air through his mouth, instead of taking it out of the water through his gills.

Now he likes to jump on a piece of weed and sit in the shade. He does not want his tail any longer, for he can swim

A FROG AND TADPOLES.

quite well with his legs. So his tail is slowly sucked in to feed his body.

There you have your little frog (4). If you look through the web of his foot at the sun, you will see that he has red blood now. But it is not warm blood like ours. He is always cold and clammy because his blood moves slowly.

He has a number of teeth in the top of his mouth, and such a curious tongue. It is tied down to the front of his mouth, and the tip, which is very sticky, lies back down his throat. He does not eat weed now. He feeds on insects and slugs. He catches them by throwing out his tongue and drawing it back very quickly.

He lives chiefly on land during the summer if he is not eaten by ducks, rats, or snakes. Then he drops to the bottom of the pond to sleep in the mud all winter.

LESSON II.

THE DRAGON-FLY AND HIS COMPANIONS.

EVERY country boy or girl, who wants to learn about water animals, should make a pond net. You have only to get a willow twig, and bind it into a hoop with string. Then make a muslin bag and sew a small stone in the bottom of it, and sew the mouth of the bag onto the hoop. Get a stick out of the hedge and fasten to it a long piece of string. Split the string near the end, and tie it to the two sides of the hoop. Then you have a net which you can let down and fish up animals from the bottom of the pond. You had better have a wide-mouthed bottle as well in which you can put what you catch. I know a shady pond just outside a farm yard at the turn of a lane. There on a bright sunny day the insects are often very busy.

In one corner of the pond the little whirligig beetles are swimming round and round, making circles in the water. Their shining black backs look almost green in the sun. Every now and then one jumps up to catch a fly in the air, or another dives down to eat a grub. Drop your net into the water and bring it up quickly under a beetle, and put him in the bottle so that you can see him.

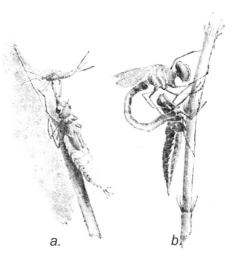

You will think that he has four eyes, for each of his two eyes is divided. One half looks up into the air, and one half looks

a. DRAGON-FLY GRUB FEEDING.
b. DRAGON-FLY CREEPING OUT OF
GRUB SKIN.

down into the water. So as he whirls about, he can see the flies in the air and the grubs in the water.

Gnats are flitting to and fro over the pond, and there is quite a crowd of those large flies with gauze wings which we call May-flies. And now a more splendid fly, three inches long, with four big gauze wings rises out of the bulrushes and flies over the pond.

All boys know the dragon-fly. His lovely wings are covered

with cross-bars filled with air, and they glitter in the sunshine with red, blue, and green colours. He has a long tail and a thick body with six legs, and a round head with huge eyes.

Each eye has more than ten thousand tiny windows in it, so that he can see up and down, right and left, as he darts about, killing the butterflies and moths that come in his way. Then he settles down on a plant or bush by the water-side, and rests till he starts off again across the pond.

If you go often in April to a pond where dragon-flies are, you may perhaps see one begin its life in the air. This is how it happens.

Under the water a large insect crawls up the stem of a plant. He has a body as big as a dragon-fly and has six legs. But he has a curious dull look in his face, and where his wings should be there are only two short stumps.

He crawls very slowly up the stem, till he comes out of the water into the air. Then a strange thing happens. The skin of his back cracks, and out creeps a real dragon-fly.

First his head, then his body with its six legs and four soft, crumpled wings, and lastly his tail. He cannot fly yet. He stands by his old empty skin, and slowly stretches out his wings to the sun. In a few hours they are long and strong and hard. Then he is ready to fly over the pond and feed.

This is how the dragon-fly comes up to the air. You will not find him so easily under the water, but we will try next week with our net. We have seen so much at the top of the pond to-day that we have not had time to dredge in the mud below.

A DRAGON-FLY.

LESSON III.

DOWN BELOW.

TO-DAY we will use our net. Hold the stick tight, and throw
the net out into the pond as a fisherman throws a fly. Then the
stone will sink the net slowly. If now you pull it gently through
the mud and water-plants, you are sure to get something.

Bring the net to land and lower it on the grass, and put all
you can find into the clear water in the bottle. You may find a
little fish, or some tadpoles, or water-snails. Or there may be
one of the curious creatures shown at a, on page 5. I'm sure
you would not think this was the grub of a dragon-fly. But it is.
It is a long insect, all joints, with six legs, and eyes something
like those of the dragon-fly. It has no wings, but a curious kind
of arm, with pincers at the end, comes out from under its chin.

This is really part of its under-lip. It is called a mask, and has
a hinge, so that it can be folded back under the chin. Now
when the grub wants food, he waits quietly in the mud, till a
beetle or a water-bug passes by. Then he throws out his mask,
and catches his prey with the pincers.

Look next at the end of its tail. Sometimes it is pointed,
sometimes it opens out like the leaves of a flower. When it is
open the grub draws water in, and uses the air in it to breathe.
Then it shoots the water out and so pushes itself across the
pond.

This dragon-fly grub lives at the bottom of the pond for
two years. So you ought to catch one some time if you try. It
changes its skin many times, and grows some wing-stumps.
Then it creeps up a stem, as we saw in the last lesson, and becomes a dragon-fly.

And now what is this in our net? At first you may think it is only a bit of stick, or a piece of mud with little stones in it, or a number of bits of grass matted together. And so it is. But there is something alive inside. If you look carefully you can see the head of an insect sticking out with six legs behind it. This

is a soft little creature called a caddis-worm. If you clear off the pieces of grass, or stick, or small stones, or shells, you will find the soft

CADDIS-GRUBS AND CADDIS-FLY.

grub inside. It has six legs and a number of little tufts under its body. It breathes with these tufts just as the tadpole does with its tufts.

You may often see caddis-worms creeping along the bottom of brooks, looking like tiny moving bundles of sticks or stones. You may pick them up without using a net. They build these cases round themselves to try to protect their soft bodies, which the fish like to eat.

By-and-by they will turn into little yellow-brown flies like moths. They rise and fall in the air over the water in the evening. We did not see them with the May-flies and gnats, because they do not like the sunshine.

You will very likely fish out a good many little water grubs in your net. But you must look carefully, for they are very small. Some have tufts all along their sides. These are the grubs of the gnats and May-flies you saw flying over the pond. They all live some time in the water. And when they come out into the air they do not live more than a few hours.

LESSON IV.

THE STICKLEBACK'S NEST.

It was a lovely day in May. The sun was shining, the grass was green, and the bushes on the banks of the river Thames were covered with fresh leaves.

In a hollow place in the river a little fish was building a nest. The fish was a stickleback. It was not more than two inches long. It had three spines sticking up on its back. Boys often catch this fish, and keep it in bottles or sell it to people who have aquariums.

It was more pleasant to watch him at work under the shade of the bushes. He brought little pieces of fine root-threads and narrow grass, and made them into a tiny saucer at the bottom of the river. Then he brought more pieces and stuck them on with slime from his mouth. In this way he made sides and a round roof. When he had done, the nest was as big as a large gooseberry.

It was about six inches below the top of the water, and had a hole right through it. When the stickleback put his head out at one end, his tail stuck out at the other. But he had not built it to live in. He wanted it for the eggs of his young ones.

He was a lovely little fish with a shining back, and bright red belly. He had a bluish green eye that shone like a jewel.

Now that his nest was built he swam off to fetch a mate. He soon came back with another fish, not so bright as himself. He played with her, and drove her, and coaxed her, till at last she went in at one hole of the nest and, after a little while, came out at the other end.

She had deposited a tiny packet of yellow eggs, which she left behind her. Then she went away and took no more care of them.

The father stickleback now went through the nest and took charge of the eggs. Each egg was not bigger than a poppy seed, and the whole bunch was very tiny. He shook the nest up and poked the eggs into a snug, safe corner. Then he swam over the top of the nest, waving his fins, so that fresh water went in and out.

STICKLEBACKS AND THEIR NEST.

Sometimes he went into the nest and brought out some dirty sand in his mouth. This he puffed away into the water. You see he wanted to keep the nest clean.

He did this every day for three weeks, till the eggs were hatched. Then a number of tiny fish came out. They were so small and transparent that you would think no other fish would see them. But the stickleback knew better. There were plenty of hungry fish watching to eat the tiny fry, which were very weak and had to carry a bag of food under their body, to suck in till they could eat.

So the brave little stickleback stuck up his three spines, and dashed angrily at any fish which snapped at his little ones. He seized their fins, and struck at their eyes and drove them away.

He made a small round place in the sand at the bottom of the river and gathered the little sticklebacks into it, and there he watched over them. Even after their spines were grown and they could swim boldly, he followed them out into the river to see that they were safe.

You may find plenty of stickleback's nests in rivers and ponds, if you look carefully for them. Or if you catch several sticklebacks in a bottle and put them in a large pan with plenty of weeds and food, most likely you will see a stickleback build his nest, and learn what a good father he is.

LESSON V.

THE KINGFISHER.

HUSH! Do not make a noise! There is a kingfisher sitting on the bough of the willow tree hanging over the river. If we once startle him, he will fly away and we shall not see him again.

How lovely he looks against the grey leaves. With his long beak and his stumpy tail he is not much larger than a sparrow, yet he seems to wear all the colours of the rainbow.

He has a bright blue streak down his back, his head and wings are a lovely green, with blue spots on the tips of the feathers. His beak is black. His chin and throat are white. He has a red streak behind his eye, with soft white feathers beyond, and his breast is shining like copper. Even his feet are red, and look quite gay against the dull branch.

He is peering down into the quiet pool under the willow, watching the fish swimming below. There! he has darted down to the water. Now he is up again with something in his mouth. It is a small minnow. He taps its head against the branch, and gulps it down, head first.

Once more, and still one more fish he catches in the same way. While he is eating the last, another kingfisher comes and perches by his side. This is his mate, who has been fishing a little way off. She is not quite so bright as he is, and has a little bit of red under her chin.

Now they are going home, and they fly away crying "Seep-seep-seep" as they go. They live in the trees and bushes by the side of the river. For you must always remember that birds do not live in nests. The nest is only a cradle for their eggs and their little ones. As soon as they are able to fly, the young birds

KINGFISHERS.

leave it with their parents, and do not often live in a nest again, till they make one for their own eggs.

I do not think you will easily find a kingfisher's nest, so I must tell you about it. When the mother wants to lay her eggs, the kingfishers dig a tunnel in the bank, and when it is made they dart into it so fast that you cannot see where they go.

But if you could know where it is and dig down from above, you would find a snug chamber which measures about six inches across. At the bottom of this chamber are a number of fish bones which the old birds have put there. They are mixed up together so that they make a nice open floor, where the wet can get away.

On the fish bones lie some shining white eggs. There will be seven, if the mother has laid as many as usual. And, if the birds are hatched, there will be seven little birds. Each bird will have all the lovely colours of which I have told you. The only difference between them and the old birds is that their beaks are shorter.

Though you may, perhaps, not find a kingfisher's nest, you will very likely see some young birds on the river. I was once out with a friend who was fishing, and while his rod was over the water, all at once two small kingfishers flew up and settled upon it. They rested a moment, and then flew on. He had only just thrown his fly again on to the water, when two more kingfishers flew up and sat on the rod. They, too, soon went on. It was clear that they were young birds just out of the nest and could not fly far.

The kingfishers are the brightest birds you can see on the river. They look so pretty among the green leaves, and hovering over the water, that if you have once seen them, you will want to see them again.

LESSON VI.

THE WATER-RAT, OR WATER-VOLE.

HAVE you ever seen a water-rat? I do not mean a land-rat swimming in the water, but a water-rat, or water vole, as he ought to be called, for he is not a true rat. I saw one once when he did not see me. What do you think he was doing? He was sitting up on his hind legs, and in his front paws he held a piece of the leaf of the sweet yellow flag, which grows so thickly by the river. It was that part of the leaf near the root which is thick and juicy. He was gnawing it so busily that he did not see me at first.

He was a stout little fellow, not quite so big as a rat. He feeds on plants. When he cannot get pieces of yellow flag he eats duckweed, or even the bark of young willows. I could see that he had a short, thick neck and round head, with a short snout. His eyes were small and I could scarcely see his ears, they were so thickly covered with fur. His round tail was not very long and had short hairs on it.

I sat down very quietly on the bank, not far from him. And presently he looked round and saw me. But as I did not move perhaps he did not think I was alive, for he went on munching his leaf.

At last I touched a dead leaf with my foot. His ears heard quickly enough. He turned his little bright eyes to me, and in a second he was in the water and swam away. I was too late to

WATER-VOLES.

see him go into his hole, but I found one not far from the flags, just under the water.

I knew I should not find his home; for the water-voles make long burrows. I went for several days to the same place, and took some bread to leave there. At last one day, as I sat watching, out came my little friend and ate the bread. After that we met several times, and he became quite tame. But I had to be very careful. The least thing frightened him, and plop he went, into the water!

If you go often to a pond or river, when all is very quiet in the evening or early morning, you may sometimes see a water-vole swimming in the water, or feeding on the bank. He has beautiful yellow teeth. The lower ones are large and show very clearly above his short lower lip.

The young water-voles are such pretty little creatures. They are born in a nest of dry grass, which the old voles make in the burrow, and when they come out they swim about with the old ones, and feed on the duckweed.

But though the water-vole lives mostly in the water, he can come on land to gather his winter store. He is often a great trouble to the farmer, for he likes the carrots and potatoes and even the broad beans, which grow in the fields, and he comes in the evening to eat them and to carry pieces back to his home.

A farmer once dug out a water-vole's burrow and found enough pieces of potato and mangold-wurzel to fill a gallon measure.

LESSON VII.

THE WATER-HEN AND THE COOT.

IF your way to school lies along a river-path, where trees hang over the water, you will very likely have seen a water-hen and her little ones. Perhaps you may know where a nest is, either among the rushes, or on a bough of a tree overhanging the water.

It is made of dead rushes, and though it is quite close to the water, it is dry and warm. If you are bathing you may look in. You will find about eight pale-grey eggs spotted with red-brown patches. Or perhaps some of the eggs may be hatched, and then the young birds will be hidden with their mother in the rushes. They are little black balls of fluff with red on their heads and white tail-feathers, and they can run and swim directly they are born. All the time you are looking, the mother, hidden in the rushes, will cry *"Crr-ook, crr-ook"* to drive you away.

She is a black bird, about as big as a pigeon, with a bright red forehead and yellow beak. And she has white feathers on the edge of her wings and under her tail. When she is in the water, she keeps jerking her head down, so that you see the white feathers, and even her green legs with their red garters.

Very soon after the young water-hens are hatched, they slip out of the nest and swim round her. If you are lying very still among the bushes, you may perhaps see them all come out on to the bank, to feed on worms or snails. Then you can notice that their feet are not webbed like a duck's feet, but all four toes are separate.

But if you make the least noise, the mother will cry *"Krek-*

MOOR-HENS AND YOUNG.

The color of the beak varies from dullest grey in the hen to gold-yellow in the cock.

BALD-HEADED COOT AND YOUNG.

krek" to her little ones, and they will dive into the water and swim to a safe place among the rushes. They will not go back to the nest, and even if you beat the rushes with a stick they will not move. They know that they are safer in their hiding place.

This bird is often called a moor-hen and she goes to the moors sometimes. But Water-hen is her better name.

And now, if there is a large lake anywhere near, you will see the water-hen there, and another bird, which you may think is the same, for she jerks her head and dives just in the same way. But if you look you will see that this second bird has not got a red forehead, but a large, bald patch on its head, and it is larger than the water-hen.

It is a bird called the coot, and often the "bald-headed coot," because of its bald patch. If you see one on the bank feeding on seeds or insects, you will notice that it has a wavy skin round each of its three front toes, though they are not joined together.

But the coot is not easy to see, for she is very shy. She runs up a tree, or dives under water, before you can get near her. She has sharp claws, which help her to climb, and which will hurt you if you catch her alive.

She builds her nest among the flags or rushes, almost touching the water. Sometimes her little ones are drowned when there is a flood.

If a boat comes near her nest, she slips off it into the rushes and cries *"Kew-kew"* to entice you away. If you find it, you will see about ten eggs in it. They are like the water-hen's eggs, but larger, and the spots are darker and smaller. If the eggs are hatched, you will know the little birds by their bald patch, though they are black, fluffy balls, just like those of the water-hen.

You will not find the coot in rivers; nor will you find her on the ponds in the winter. Then she starts off with a number of other coots to the sea in the south of England, and stays till spring comes again.

LESSON VIII.
THE WATER-BUGS.

WHEN you go home from school, if you pass a pond, you are almost sure to be able to find one, or more, of the three water-bugs of this lesson, and I want you to look at them.

The first is a long, thin, black insect. He walks on top of the water, looking like a needle on legs. He is sometimes called a "needle-bug," but more often a "water-measurer," because he seems to measure the water with his legs as he runs.

He has very fine hairs under his body and on his legs. The air between these hairs prevents him from getting wet and being drowned. He has two long feelers, and a long thin beak. His legs and body are a reddish colour and his wings a glossy black.

If you watch him, you will see him start all at once across the pond. He is catching a water-fly. Then he will hold it in his front claws, and suck the juice out of its body. Though the water-measurer has wings, he does not often fly.

The next water-bug is not so thin. He is about an inch long, and has a flat body with grey wings folded across it. He has only very short feelers, and his front legs are thick and strong, with pincers at the end, and this is why he is called the "water-scorpion." He uses these pincers to seize the insects in the water, and sucks them dry through his sharp beak.

He swims under water very slowly, or crawls in the mud, and is easily caught. You may catch him too when he comes up to get air. This he does in a very funny way. He has two long bristles at the end of his tail. When he puts these together they make a tube like a hollow straw. He comes near the top of the water, and thrusts out the end of this tube into the air, and draws some into his body. The eggs of the mother water-scorpion are stuck on to the leaves of water-plants, and look like seeds.

a. WATER-SCORPION.
b. WATER-BOATMAN.
c. WATER-MEASURER.

The last water-bug I am sure you know. He is a little fellow, rather like a beetle, with six legs, two of them being very long ones; and he swims upside down, rowing himself along with these two legs, as if they were oars. This is why he is called a "water-boatman."

He has a long, sucking beak, but you will hardly see it unless you dip him out with a glass and look close. For as he swims upside-down, the bug bends his head down on his chest, so that his beak lies between his legs.

His eyes at the side of his head are very large, so that he can look both down and up. This is very useful, for he swims under tadpoles and grubs, and catches them in his claws. Then he bites them with his sharp beak, and sucks out their soft body. He is always swimming in the water, or crawling in the mud. In the evening he sometimes comes out and flies to another pond or ditch.

The mother water-boatman lays small, long, white eggs on stems and leaves in the water. You may often find them in March, and in April you may see the little bugs swimming upside down like their parents.

If you take the trouble, you may catch these three water-bugs in a net, and put them in a glass, and see all I have told you.

LESSON IX.
ALONG THE RIVER.

LET us stroll a short distance along the river. How pretty it is, with the evening sun shining through the trees! What a number of little creatures are enjoying themselves in the air and in the water!

Pale little Tommy, who has come from London for a holiday, slips his hand in mine and says, "I wish I could live in the country." When he goes back to his own home in a narrow street, where there is only a hard pavement instead of green grass, and no shady trees nor flowing water, he will remember this walk by the river.

Look at those fish, about three inches long, swimming up
and down under the bridge. Those are bull-heads. They are
called so because they have such broad, thick heads. And they
have a sharp spine on each side of their head, which we might
call the bull's horns. You will feel those spines if you try to hold
them in your hand. The kingfisher knows them well enough,
if he tries to swallow one, for they stick in his throat.

BULL-HEAD (MILLER'S THUMB) AND MAY-FLIES.

You boys call them "miller's thumbs." I wonder why you
think that millers have broad thumbs? The bull-heads hide under stones, and eat water insects, and the eggs of other fish. Ah!
Fred has caught one and put it in the bottle. Now Tommy can
see what a lovely eye the bull-head has, and the red, green,
brown and yellow colours on his scales.

How busy those flies are with long wings and three long
bristles on their tails. They are May-flies rising and falling over

the water. They are not feeding, for May-flies do not eat, and only live a few hours. But they have lived a long time under water as grubs, like the dragon-fly grub. They only want now to lay their eggs and die.

The gnats flying over that quiet pool near the mill are quite different. One has just pricked my hand and sucked some blood, so I know that he can feed. But then gnats have not had so long a life in the water as the May-flies.

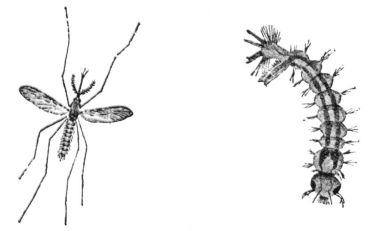

GNAT AND GNAT GRUB.

Those gnats flying over the pool were only born a few weeks ago. Their mother laid some sticky eggs, each not bigger than the point of a pin, and left them in a packet on the top of the still water. They were very soon hatched, and a number of grubs came out, looking like very tiny worms with fine hairs on their sides. Each swam about in the water and ate specks of weed.

Why do you think they swam with their heads down? Because they could only breathe near their tails, and so had to stick them up in the air.

In about three weeks each grub had changed his skin three times. The fourth time he came out with a wrapper round him, and if you could have looked at him then, you would have seen a perfect gnat, with wings, cuddled up inside.

Now he had to creep out, and that was very risky. For if he fell in the water he would be drowned. So he stretched himself very carefully on the top of the pool, and began to push his head through a slit in the wrapper.

Then he drew himself gently out, and stood on tiptoe on the empty skin, which floated like a boat on the water. He spread his wings, and then he was safe and flew away. Sometimes the wind blows him over before he can get out, and then he is drowned.

If you take a pail of water out of a pond in May, and keep it in the open air, you may be able to see a gnat grow up, for there will most likely be a great many in it. But you must have sharp eyes, for they are very tiny.

And now the sun is setting and birds and beasts and flowers are all going to rest. Soon the night-moths and the owls and bats will be coming out. We must go home.

LESSON X.

THE OTTER FAMILY.

ABOUT five o'clock one fine morning in May, Tom, the gamekeeper's son, was examining the traps set for weasels, stoats, and other vermin. His way led him over a bridge across the river, and as he came near it he heard a strange whistling noise.

Now Tom was a Devonshire lad, and all country boys in the

West of England have sharp ears for the calls of animals. Tom knew that this cry came from a father or mother otter who were fishing in the river with their little ones.

Just below the bridge, where the bank was very high, there grew an old willow tree, with branches hanging over the river. The water had washed away the bank under the willow, so that there was a big hole between its strong roots.

Now Tom knew that this hole was the home of some otters. Many a time the otter-hounds had stood in the water near this hole baying with all their might. But they could not get in, and the otters took care not to come out.

The hounds were far away now, and everything was very quiet in the early morning. So Tom lay down in the thick grass at the top of the bank and waited. By-and-bye on came the otters, swimming smoothly along with only their noses above water.

The old otters swam so quietly that Tom would not have known they were there. But the young otters were playing and twisting about, so that first their brown furry backs, and then their white bellies, shone in the light of the early morning sun, and the water splashed about them.

The river was very broad in this place, and just opposite the willow was a small island. Tom was so well hidden in the tall grass that the otters had no idea that he was there. So one by one they scrambled up on the island, each with a fish in its mouth. Then they each took hold of their fish with their front feet, and began to eat just behind the head. They ate on till they nearly reached the tail and then left that.

While they were eating, Tom could see what they were like.

OTTER EATING FISH.

They had long bending bodies, and broad, flat heads, and their mouths and noses were short and broad. Their feet were webbed like duck's feet, but each foot had very sharp claws at the end. Their fur was a lovely soft brown, but the long hairs on the old otters were coarse, and they did not look so soft as the little ones. Their tails were thick and strong, and very useful for helping them to swim.

The father tore the fish with his teeth quite fiercely, and sometimes threw small pieces to the young ones, who had soon finished their tiny fish. At last all was eaten up, except the heads and tails. Then the father otter slid down the bank, and the others followed him, and they all went to fish again.

There are fewer otters than there used to be in the rivers of England. But they are still to be found in many places. Only, if you want to see them at home, you must get up early in the morning.

LESSON XI.
FLOWERS FOR THE SHOW.

"Where are you going, Peggy?" asked Peter, as he passed her in the lane, one Saturday afternoon in July.

"I am going to look for flowers, for the flower-show next week. I shall not gather them, but I want to see what I can find."

"May I go with you?"

"Yes, if you can keep a secret. I want to make quite a new kind of nosegay, of flowers that grow in the water."

"But they will all fade if you put them in a bunch."

"I am not going to put them in a bunch. I am going to get

one of father's large zinc pans which he uses for the dogs' food, and let the plants float in the water."

So Peggy and Peter started off to their favourite pond.

"See, Peter, I must have one of those lovely yellow 'water-lilies,' with its large, shiny green leaf, and one of its curious seed-boxes, which remain after the yellow flower-leaves have fallen off. I know that this plant has a thick stem in the mud at the bottom of the pond, and the long stalks grow right up, so that the leaves float on the top of the water. Little beetles crawl inside the flower and get honey from under the small yellow flower-leaves inside.

"Then I must have some of those white stars with yellow in the middle. They look so pretty among their small green leaves, which are cut into three half-rounds. That is the 'water-crow-foot,' and if you hook a bit in with your stick we shall see that it has some other leaves under water, which are cut into strips like fine blades of grass."

"Why should it have two kinds of leaves, Peggy?"

"One set are its floating leaves to keep the flowers above the water, where the insects can get at them, and the others are lighter and can spread out in the water without making so much green leaf. And look, Peter, the yellow lines on the white flowers point straight to the narrow end of the flower-leaf, where the insects find the honey.

"Then I must have some duckweed. It will cover the pan so nicely."

"But the duckweed is not pretty, Peggy. It is all leaves."

"No, Peter, that is just what it is not. Paul told me the other day that the duckweed has no real leaves. Each plant is a little

WHITE AND YELLOW WATER-LILIES.

bit of stem with a thin root hanging down in the water. Very tiny flowers sometimes grow in a little split in the side of the stem. I shall try to get one of these, but they are so very small, and are only made of two little dust-bags and a seed-box. But the duckweed will float on the water.

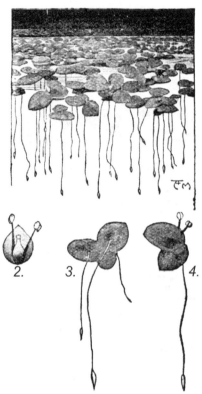

"Now, Peter, I want to find a 'bog-bean' in flower. I am afraid it is rather late in the year, but there are some, I know, at the shallow end of the pond. You must look for a large spike of pink-white flowers, shaped something like

1. DUCKWEED. 2,4. DUCKWEED FLOWERS. 3. ATTACHMENT OF THE ROOTS.

wide blue-bells and lined with a number of white hairs. Ah! here is one with the buds just opening; it will be all right for Wednesday.

"Now we must have one more. A little plant called the 'water-milfoil,' which is almost all under water, except the spike of tiny pink flowers which stands straight up in the air. Look at its fine leaves arranged in stars round the stem. They lie out so well in the water. If you look very carefully at the flowers, you will see that the top ones have only dust-bags in them, and the lower ones have only seed-boxes. But they are so small it is not easy to see this.

"Now I must not choose any more, for I must describe each one on my show-card, and it will take a long time."

LESSON XII.

PEGGY'S WATER-PLANTS.

WHEN Wednesday came, Peggy's pan was ready. She had taken it to the pond and dipped it gently under the duckweed. She brought it up quite full, and picked it over very carefully, leaving only the best plants. Then she carried it to the show-room.

There she put the yellow lily into the middle of the pan, so that the flower, and the stalk with the seed-vessel, fitted into the hollow between the ears of the large green leaf just at the leaf-stalk. Next she put pieces of the water-crowfoot here and there, the pretty white blossoms streaked with yellow resting upon the top of the water.

She stuck two spikes of bog-bean, with their leaves, one on each side of the water-lily. Lastly, she put spikes of the water-milfoil round the edge of the pan. Their leaves made little green stars in the water all the way round, and their tiny pink flower-spikes made a lovely edge.

Then she wrote her card. This is what she said:

1. The yellow water-lily grows in the pond near the farm. It has a thick stem rooted in the mud down at the bottom. I saw it once when they cleaned the pond. We see nothing on top of the water in March. But in May the large shining green leaves

have grown to the top of the water on long stalks. They are shaped rather like a heart, but are pointed at the tip.

In June the buds come up. They are like green knobs tipped with yellow. But as they grow bigger, the five outer leaves, or *sepals*, open, and they are quite yellow inside. Then we can see the small inner flower-leaves, or *petals*, arranged in two rows; after them come a number of *stamens*, made of thin threads, with dust-bags on the top. Then right in the middle is the seed-box, or *ovary*. It is shaped like a water-bottle with a round cushion on the top, and has a number of sticky points, which lie on the cushion in the shape of a star. Little beetles are often found in the flowers. They fly in, and suck the honey at the back of the petals.

2. The water-crowfoot grows in our pond. It is a kind of buttercup. It has five outer green

WATER-BUTTERCUP,
WITH IT'S TWO
KINDS OF LEAVES.

leaves, or sepals. They turn back against the stem when the flower is open. They often fall off. There are five white petals. They are streaked with yellow near the middle of the flower, where there are drops of honey. After the petals, come many stamens, and then, in the middle of the flower, a number of seed-boxes, each with one seed inside.

The water-crowfoot has two kinds of leaves. The leaves which float on top of the water are flat and cut into three half rounds. The leaves under water are cut into threads and spread out on all sides.

3. There is a great deal of duck-weed in our pond. Each plant has one little root in the water and a kind of stem at the top. It has no leaves. The tiny flowers sometimes come out of a slit in the side of the stem. Each flower is nothing but two dust-spikes and a tiny seed-box.

WATER MILFOIL.

4. The bog-bean, or buck-bean, is nearly out of flower now. It grows at the edge of the pond, and its leaves are cut into three long parts. The pinkish flowers stand out on little stalks

upon a tall stem. They are cup-shaped, with five points, and have a number of white hairs inside.

5. The water-milfoil grows almost all under water. Only the small pink flowers stand in a spike out in the air. The flowers at the top of the spike have only stamens in them. Lower down some have both dust-bags and seed-boxes. The ones at the bottom have seed-boxes, or ovaries, only. Milfoil leaves are narrow, like grass, but quite short. They stand round the stem like the spokes of a wheel, or the rays of a star.

Peggy's water-nosegay and show-card won the prize.

BOOK III
PLANT LIFE IN FIELD AND GARDEN

"EYES AND NO EYES"

Third Book.

PLANT LIFE IN FIELD AND GARDEN.

LESSON I.
THE SHEPHERD'S PURSE.

IT is seven o'clock on a lovely summer morning. Jump up and look out of the window. It is a shame to be in bed when the sun is shining so brightly, and the birds are singing, and the bees are flying from flower to flower.

Why are the bees at work so early? They want to gather the yellow pollen-dust from the flowers, and the dew helps them to wet it, so that they can roll it up in little balls. Then they pack these balls into a groove in their hind legs, and fly away to the hive. There they mix it with honey, and make it into bee-bread to feed the young bees.

See how busy that woodpecker is, under the elm tree. He is catching insects to carry home to his little ones, which have been hatched more than a week. Further away in the field is a thrush struggling with a big worm: I expect that he too is getting a breakfast for his family.

How busy they all are, and you in bed! If I were you I would get up and pull up some weeds in the garden. Then you will be of some use, and you can learn many interesting things, while you are at work.

Here is a weed, growing among the cabbages. Do you know its name? It is called "The Shepherd's Purse" because of its curious seed-pods. These grow on stalks up the stem of the plant, below the little white flowers. If you open one of them very carefully, you will find that there is a small bag on each side, which can be pulled away from the middle, when the pod is ripe, leaving the seeds hanging on a small division.

So the pod is a kind of purse, with two pockets, and we can pretend that the seeds are the shepherd's money.

Take hold of this plant, and I will tell you about its different parts. First look at the root. That always grows downwards into the ground. It has small rootlets growing out of it. The root and the rootlets all have tender tips, and they drink in the food of the plant out of the ground.

You know that your father puts manure into the earth before he sows his seeds, or plants his fruit trees. Then the rain sinks into the earth and takes the juice out of the manure. This makes a, rich drink for the roots to suck in, and so the plants grow strong.

Next look at the stem. You can tell where it begins, for a tuft of leaves grows close to the ground. A root never has any leaves on it, so where the leaves grow must be the stem. The place where the stem joins the root is often called the stock.

Look carefully at this tuft of leaves. You will see that they do not grow exactly one above the other. The leaves in the upper row always grow just between the leaves of the lower row. And

SHEPHERD'S PURSE.

as the stem grows upwards, and the leaves are farther apart, they still grow so that they are not exactly one above the other.

Why do you think they grow like this? Because they want to get as much sun as they can. If they grew exactly one above the other, the upper leaf would keep the sun away from the lower one. But now they get as much as there is to be had.

You see then that a plant has a root which grows downwards to take in water out of the ground, and stems to grow upwards and carry the leaves up into the sunlight. What the leaves do we will learn in the next lesson.

LESSON II.
THE WORK DONE BY LEAVES.

The leaves want a great deal of sunshine and air, for they are busy all day long, making food. Have you ever thought how wonderful it is that plants can make their own food? You do not make your food, and no animals make their own food. All you eat has once been either an animal or a plant. In a cake, for instance, the flour comes from grains of wheat, the currants from a little tree, the sugar from the sugar-cane, the spices come from trees, and the candied peel from fruits.

The other things you eat are meat, fish, birds, vegetables, and fruits, and all these have once been alive.

Plants do not feed like this. Their roots take in water out of the earth, and other substances, such as lime, soda, and potash, dissolved in it. The leaves take in gases out of the air. But earth, air, and water are not living food. You or I could not live on them. The plant can.

The pretty green leaves we love so much work very hard.

When the sun shines upon them they can turn the water and gases into living food, and this food makes more leaves, flowers, and fruits which we eat.

See how useful plants are! If they did not make food, there could be nothing alive in the world. Insects feed on plants, and birds feed on insects. Sheep feed on grass, and we feed on sheep. Rabbits feed on plants, and foxes and weasels feed on rabbits. If there were no plants, there could be no insects, no birds, no animals, and no men alive.

But this is not the only useful work which plants do. You know that if many people are shut up in a room, they use up the fresh air, and breathe back bad air, which is not fit to use again. Now plants want this foul air. They take it in through their leaves, and use a gas which is in it to help them to grow. So they not only turn gases into food for us to eat, but in doing this they use the bad air we send out of our mouths, and give it back to us fresh and pure. This is why it is so healthy to live in the country, where there are so many plants.

You will find it very interesting to look at the leaves of plants, and notice their shapes, and how they are arranged on their stems so as to get light and air.

I think you must know the common Dead-nettle, which is so like a stinging-nettle but does not sting. It grows in the hedges, and has a pretty purple or white flower shaped like a hood. Its leaves are arranged in pairs all up the stem, and each pair stands exactly across the pair below it, so as to let in plenty of light.

The glossy green leaves of the ivy on the wall lie out flat, and have long stalks, so that they can stand out well into the air.

The leaves of the Nasturtiums in our gardens are shaped like a round shield. The leaf-stalk grows from under the middle of the leaf and is very long. So the leaf looks up straight to the sky, and gets plenty of light and air.

The leaf of the Horse Chestnut tree is divided into leaflets, so that it looks as if it were made of five leaves, and each leaflet is spread out to the light.

a. DEAD-NETTLE.
b. WOOD SORREL.

The leaves of the little Wood Sorrel, which children love to bite because it tastes sour, have three round leaflets like the Shamrock, and these leaflets droop down at night, or on a wet day, but stand up wide open when the sun is shining.

And now let us go back to our shepherd's purse. We have not yet looked for the flowers; they grow on stalks which come out between the leaf-stalks and the stem. On these stalks there are some smaller leaves and a good many seed-pods.

Above the seed-pods at the top of the stalk are some white flowers growing close together. They are so small that you can scarcely see the parts. But you can make out that they have four outer green leaves and four white inner leaves. In the next lesson we will learn more about these.

Gather six plants with different shaped leaves and notice how they grow upon the stem.

LESSON III.

THE STORY OF A TURNIP.

THE flowers of the Shepherd's Purse are very small, so we will get the flowers of another plant to help us to learn about them. If you can find, in the garden, a turnip plant that has run to seed, you will see that it has flowers very like those of the Shepherd's Purse, only they are larger, and yellow instead of white.

In both flowers there are four outer green leaves. These are called *sepals*. They form the cup or *calyx* of the flower. Then there are the four coloured leaves, which grow above the sepals. These are called *petals*. They make the crown or *corolla* of the flower. They are white in the Shepherd's Purse, and yellow in the Turnip flower. But in both flowers they stand in the form of a cross.

Next come six thin threads with little knobs on the top. Two of them are short, and four are long. These are called *stamens*. The knobs are called *anthers*, they are the dust-bags which hold the yellow dust or *pollen*. Lastly, in the middle of the flower, is the seed-box or *ovary*. In the Shepherd's Purse the ovary is shaped like a heart, in the Turnip flower it is a long pod.

The pods grow on little stalks down the stem. They once had flower-leaves round them. But these have withered away, and the pods have grown large.

Some of the best vegetables in your garden have flowers like these in the form of a cross, and with four long and two short stamens. Some, like the turnip and radish, have roots that are good to eat. In others, such as the cabbage and mustard-and-cress, we eat the leaves. In cauliflower and broccoli we eat the flowers.

Now let us go back to our turnip. What a splendid round root it has! You can find a kind of turnip growing wild in the lanes, but the root is hard—you would not like to eat it. Our turnips are good, because they have been grown in good ground, and had good food for hundreds of years, and only the best seeds are sown.

Now I daresay you think that, as we dig the ground and sow the seed, we ought to keep the turnip for ourselves. But there are a good many animals and insects which want their share. As soon as the turnip seed has sent up its first green leaves, a little beetle is there, ready to eat them. When its wings are closed it is not much bigger than the letter O in the title of this lesson. It has long hind legs and can hop very far, so it is called the Turnip Flea-beetle.

In the winter these beetles sleep under the clods of earth, or under dead leaves. When spring comes they wake up, and feed on the Shepherd's Purse, or some other weed, which comes up early in the year. The mother flea-beetle lays her eggs under the leaves, and very soon the tiny maggots come out, and eat tunnels in them.

In a fortnight they are fat. Then they fall to the ground, and wrap themselves up in their cocoon skin, just as the baby ants

did in the ant-hill. In another fortnight they become little beetles.

By that time the early turnips are just sending up their first
leaves, and the flea-beetles will hop a long way to eat them. So,
when you get up some morning, you may find the turnip bed
very bare, and if you have sharp eyes you may catch the little

GARDEN AND TURNIP AND FLEA-BEETLE.
Parts of the Flower: s. Sepal   *p.* Petal   *d.* Dust-bags or Anthers.
o. Ovary or Seed-pod.
1. Flea-beetle Grub.   *2.* Beetle Flying. (Both much enlarged.)

black shiny beetles which have done the mischief. A whole field of swedes or yellow turnips may be eaten down in this way.

If you clear away all the weeds early in the year, and rake the ground, so that the young turnips grow quickly, you may keep the flea-beetle away. But then other creatures are wanting their share. The turnip-weevil will lay her egg in the root underground, as the nut-weevil did in the nut in the tree (see Book I.). If you pull up a turnip with little lumps or galls on it, you may know that a weevil maggot has been hatched inside.

Then, when the large turnip leaves have grown, the pretty orange saw-fly will leave her eggs in them, so that the maggots eat them all away. Then the rabbit, if he can get in, will eat the tops, while the mice will nibble at the root. Lastly, if you grow turnips for seed, the pretty little green flower-beetle wants his share, and he eats the flower-buds.

So you see the turnips feed many creatures besides the sheep and ourselves. A good gardener enjoys learning how to keep these garden thieves away.

Bring the flowers of wallflower, stock, candytuft, penny-cress, turnip-flower, and shepherd's purse, and notice their likeness in the form and arrangement of their parts.

LESSON IV.
HOW A SEED GROWS.

WE saw in the last two lessons that a plant has a root, stem, leaves, flowers, and seed-boxes. To-day I want to tell you how these grow.

If your teacher will let you make a little experiment, you can watch a plant yourself as it grows out of the seed. Get a saucer and a small piece of flannel. Put the flannel in the saucer, and pour water over it till it is quite wet. Then get someone to give you a pinch of mustard seed, and scatter it on the flannel. Put this on the windowsill, or on the table, and take care to keep the flannel wet. Then watch what happens.

The second day after you have sown the seeds, you will find that they are swollen and soft. They have sucked up some water, and are using it to grow. On the third day many of the seeds will have sent out a tiny white root, which will cling to the flannel.

The tip of the root will now suck in more water, and if you will open a seed you will find that it is splitting in half. Each of the two halves is going to be a leaf. But they are not green, they are still quite white, and you would not think that they were leaves.

When you go to school on the fourth morning you may find these two halves out of their coat. Some of them are white, but some are turning green above and purple below, and everyone would now call them leaves. They grow up on a stem, and the empty coat of the seed still hangs on the place where the stem and the root meet. Look well at the shape of these leaves, they are made of two rounds with a dent in the middle. They are the seed-leaves of the mustard plant. They have come out of the seed, and have used the food that was in it, to spread themselves out, and rise up into the sunlight. Now as the light pours down on them, they turn green, and can make their own food out of the water and gases, which the roots suck in. For the root has now many rootlets and root-hairs on it, as you will see if you will pull one out of the flannel.

In a few days a green tip shows between the two seed-leaves, and grows up, opening out into two more leaves. These again have a little bud growing between them, which spreads out into other leaves, and so the plant goes on getting larger.

But the new leaves are quite different in shape from the seed-leaves. They are long, and are cut up into five leaflets, one large one at the tip, and two small ones on each side.

What you have seen happen to the mustard seed on the flannel is just what happens to every seed you sow in the ground. First it swells, when the warm rain reaches it. Then it puts out a tiny root. The seed-leaves stretch themselves out, their stem grows, and they creep out of their coat, and find their way above ground.

There they turn green in the sunlight, and begin to work up nourishing food. With this food they make fresh stems and leaves, till they grow into big plants, or even trees.

Another pretty experiment you can make is to soak a haricot bean in warm water, and put it on the top of some earth in a pot. Keep the earth moist and watch the bean, as you did the mustard seed. It will take longer to grow. It may be nearly a week before the root finds its way into the earth, and another week before the big green seed-leaves break out of the seed-coat.

It is very curious to watch the root. First it sends out only one rootlet. Then several more grow out, till the bean looks like a big spider with long legs. The heavy bean still lies on the earth, while the stem goes on growing. So the stem forms an

A BEAN GROWING.

1. Soaked Seed. *2.* Root Appearing. *3.* Arched stem before the seed-leaves rise up. *4.* Seed-leaves open with shoots between.
5. Full-grown Bean-plant.

arch, with the seed at one end, and the root at the other. At last the seed-leaves grow thinner as the plant uses the food in them, and the stem is strong enough to lift them, so that they stand up in the air. They do not leave the seed-coat down below, as the mustard seed did. They carry it up with them, and it dries and falls off at the top. Then you can see the new bud, between the seed-leaves, which soon opens out into real leaves.

Grow mustard seed on damp flannel. Soak a haricot bean in warm water for one night, and then keep it on very damp earth in a flower-pot.

LESSON V.

MAKING NEW SEEDS.

W<small>E</small> left our plants, at the end of the last lesson, growing green leaves in the sunlight. Now they go on very quickly. Their roots take in water from the ground, and the leaves take in gases from the air.

When the plant has made plenty of roots, stems, and leaves, it begins to store up food for making flowers, in which new seeds will be formed. This is a very important work, for seeds are needed to grow up into new plants, and so many are destroyed by birds and insects or stifled by other plants that, if there were not plenty, the plants would die out.

So the seed-box, or ovary, is very carefully protected. It grows right in the middle of the flower, where it can be closely

wrapped up in the bud. Even when it grows below the flower, as in the honeysuckle, the sticky tip is always safe inside the bud.

BUTTERCUP.

1. Flower. *2.* fruit with separate seed-boxes or Ovaries (*o.*) *3.* Seed-box cut open to show Seed.

Gather a Primrose and Buttercup in the field, and a flower from the row of Peas in the garden, and look for their seed-boxes. In the middle of the butter-cup flower you will find a great number, shaped like pears standing upside down, with their stalks upwards, and in each of these seed-boxes there is the beginning of a little seed.

You will have to pull the yellow crown off the Primrose before you can see the little round seed-box sitting in the green cup. It has a tube growing out of it with a round knob on the top.

In the Pea-flower you will find one single pod inside the flower-leaves, and it has a long beak on the tip. When you open the pod you will see seven or eight white balls inside it, which are

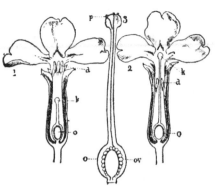

PIMROSE FLOWERS.

1. Flower with Anthers (*a*) high up and sticky knob (*k*) in the tube.

2. Flower with Anthers (*a*) high up and sticky knob (*k*) high up; (*o*)ovary.

3. Ovary (*o*) with ovules (*ov*) and pollen (*p*) growing down to them.

the baby peas. If you can cut open the seed-box of the primrose, you will find the same kind of balls, but very small indeed. These balls are soft and transparent. You can crush them with your fingers easily. They are not yet real seeds, but only bags of juice, called "ovules." Before they can grow into hard seeds, they must use some of the yellow grains out of the dust-bags which grow round them.

This is why the seed-boxes have tips, and beaks and knobs. The tip of the buttercup pods, the beak at the end of the pea-pod, and the knob at the top of the primrose-tube, are all sticky. The yellow grains stick to them like flies on fly-paper. Then the grains burst and send some juice down to the ovules in the seed-box, and turn them into real hard seeds.

As you go home pick any flower you see, and try to find its seed-box. You may perhaps pick a Poppy in the cornfield. That has a fine large seed-box, like a covered cup, with holes under the cover. When the seed-box is ripe, and hangs down its head, the seeds fall out at the holes. There are so many you could not count them.

You may pick a Violet, and when you have taken off the coloured leaves, you will find a very curious seed-box. For the tube, and the sticky knob at the top, are just like a bird's neck and head. The dust-bags which fit close round the seed-box are a lovely orange colour.

If you can find a pretty purple flower called the Marsh Mallow, you will see that the seed-box is like a round flat cheese, with a long tube standing up in the middle. This tube has eight or twelve red sticky points; there are a great many yellow stamens round it. Country children often call the seed-boxes of the mallow "cheeses," when they are ripe and the long tube has fallen off.

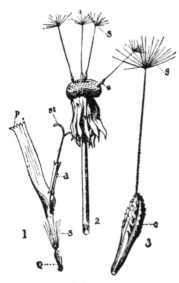

PARTS OF A DANDELION.

1. A single Flower: (*s*) Sepals; (*p*) Petals; (*st*) sticky horns; (*a*) Anthers; (*o*) Ovary.
2. Cushion on which the Flowers grow. Four Fruits are left on it: (*s*) Sepals; (*o*) Ovary.
3. Enlarged Fruit with (*s*) Sepals; (*o*) Ovary.

But very likely you may pick a Daisy or a Dandelion. Then you will be puzzled, for you will not find a seed-box in the middle. This is because a daisy or a dandelion is not one flower, but a great many flowers crowded together in one head.

DANDELION.

Take a dandelion flower-head to pieces, and you will find that each tiny flower will come away from the rest. There are more than a hundred in one dandelion head. Take one of these florets in your hand and have a look at it. At the bottom there is an oval bag, that is the seed-box. On the top of it there are some fine hairs, these are the sepals. Then there is the yellow crown with a long strap to it. Inside the crown come the stamens, with very long dust-bags, which cling round the tube. On the top of the tube stand two yellow sticky horns.

So you see this tiny thing is a whole flower, growing with its companions on the dandelion head. The daisy is the same, with some little differences. See if you can make that out for yourself.

Find the seed-boxes of the pea, wallflowers, shepherd's purse, buttercup, primrose, poppy, marsh-mallow, and dandelion.

LESSON VI.
HOW INSECTS HELP.

As soon as the sun begins to warm the earth you may look out for spring flowers. If you have any damp ditches near you, you may find in March the Marsh Marigold in flower. This is a plant with hollow stems and dark green leaves shaped like a heart, and notched round the edge. It has large bright yellow flowers, which children often call "king-cups."

The yellow cup has only one set of flower-leaves. and inside it there are a great many dust-bags and seed-boxes. If you take off one of these seed-boxes and look on each side, you will find a little hollow with some honey in it.

The bees are very eager to get this honey, as it is so early in the year that there are very few plants in flower. They want too some of the pollen dust to make bee-bread for the baby-bees. The early flies too are in search of food. If you watch a bed of king-cups on a sunny day, you will see a number of bees and flies settling on the flowers.

They fly from flower to flower sipping a drop in each, and as they rub against the dust-bags, they carry the pollen-grains with them.

We saw in the last lesson that plants cannot make seeds unless the pollen grows downwards into the seed-box, and we find by experiments that they make better seeds when the pollen-grains come from another flower. So the bees do the flowers good, by carrying the pollen, in return for the honey that the plants give to them.

You are sure to find somewhere in the lanes in March a pretty little yellow flower like a star, with shining heart-shaped green leaves. It is the Lesser Celandine, and has a cup of five green sepals, and a crown of eight or ten yellow petals. Flies and bees come to it in numbers, for it has a drop of honey at the thin end of each petal, in the middle of the crown.

If you dig up a bit of this plant, you will find some white lumps growing among the roots. Each of these has a small bud at the top, and will grow into a plant if you put it into the ground.

Another flower already out in the fields is the common yellow Coltsfoot, a very tiresome weed to the farmers. It has a long creeping stem, and spreads very quickly underground. It has a flower-head, like the dandelion, made of hundreds of tiny flowers. This head grows on a fluffy stem which is covered with pink scales. The leaves do not grow till after the flowers are over.

Look carefully at the flower-head. You will find about forty tiny round flowers in the middle. They have dust-bags in them, and a large drop of honey. Round these stand about three hundred little flowers, each with a long yellow strap, and inside each of these outer flowers is a seed-box with two sticky horns. The bees and flies creep over these outer florets to suck the honey from the flowers in the middle, and on their way back they bring some pollen and leave it on the sticky horns.

And now, if you can find in the hedges the Cuckoo-pint or Arum I will show you a real trap for insects. It is a plant with a green pointed hood, and a purple club sticking up in the middle. We used to call it "Lords and Ladies," but many children call it "Parson-in-the-pulpit." In spring this plant has a very strong smell. When the flies smell it, they crawl down the purple club to look for honey.

On their way they pass a row of stiff hairs (1, p. 22) which bend down with their weight and let them pass. Then they come to a ring of red dust-bags (2) which are not yet open. Next they pass some useless seed-boxes (3) and reach at last the true seed-boxes (4) with sticky points.

Now they have come to the bottom, and they look for some honey. Alas! There is none there. Then they try to get back. But the stiff hairs will not bend upwards, and they are prisoners. They are shut in for a day or two, and then the sticky points of the seed-boxes wither, and each gives out a drop of honey. So the flies have not been cheated. At the same time the

MARSH MARIGOLD.

1. ARUM OR CUCKOO-PINT.

1A. FLOWERING STEM.

   1. Stiff hairs.   2. Anthers or Dust-bags.
   3. Useless Ovaries.   4. True Ovaries.

2. THE COLTSFOOT.

dust-flags burst, and the pollen dust falls on the flies. Then the stamens and the hairs wither away and the flies can get out again.

As they pass the withered dust-bags, they brush off any pollen-grains which remain, and have plenty on their backs to carry to another flower-trap.

You can see this for yourself if you will look for the Parson-in-the-pulpit, and choose two plants, one young one with the dust-bags full, and one old one in which they are withered.

Look for marsh marigold, lesser celandine, coltsfoot, and arum or cuckoo-pint.

LESSON VII.

SEED-BOXES WHICH WE EAT AS VEGETABLES.

WHEN the seed-boxes of plants are ripe we call them "fruits." I daresay it seems strange to you to call a pea-pod a fruit. But if you think of all the other fruits you know, you will find that they are all seed-boxes.

The apple is the seed-box of the apple-blossom. The gooseberry holds the seed of the gooseberry plant. The nut is the fruit of the nut-tree. The acorn is the fruit of the oak.

In peas and broad beans we eat the seeds out of the fruit. But in French beans and scarlet-runners we eat the whole fruit, seed-box as well as seeds. If you walk round a kitchen garden I think you can find one, and perhaps two, vegetables of which we eat the whole fruit.

In most gardens there is some corner where the dead leaves and rubbish are heaped up to make a hot-bed. Earth is thrown over the heap, and cucumbers and vegetable marrows are grown there. You will see at once that cucumbers and marrows are fleshy seed-boxes, for they are full of seeds.

Have you ever looked at the flowers of the Vegetable Marrow? They are as large and beautiful as many garden flowers. I want you to notice something curious in them.

If you look at several flowers you will see that they are not all alike. They all have a pale green cup, with five long points, and a grand yellow crown. But some, which are very big, have the beginning of a young marrow just under the green cup while others, which are smaller, have nothing but the stem under the cup. In a few days the young marrow will have grown

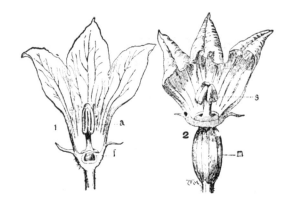

VEGETABLE MARROW FLOWERS.
1. Flower with (*a*) Anthers and (*f*) juicy folds.
2. Flower which bears the (*m*) Marrow with it's sticky (*s*) Stigma.

bigger. But the flowers which have no marrows under them will be fading away.

Look inside the fading flowers. You will see some curious twisted pouches full of yellow pollen-dust, but you will not find a sticky knob in the middle. Then look at the big flower at the top of the young marrow. Inside that flower you will find some sticky lumps, and most likely some yellow dust on them. So you will know that these lumps are the top of the seed-box. But you will not find any dust-bags in this flower.

So you see that the vegetable marrow has its dust-bags in one flower and its seed-box in another. How can the yellow grains get from one flower to the other to make the seeds grow?

Here the insects help. We found them troublesome when they spoilt the turnips, but now, they are going to be useful.

Inside each marrow flower there are some juicy folds, which the bees and flies love to nibble, to get the sweet juice. When they press into the flower to bite the folds they rub against the pouches and carry off some yellow grains on their backs. Then they go into the bigger flower to bite the folds, and pass the sticky lumps on their way. The yellow grains stick on to the lumps, and so the ovules of the marrow get the pollen-food and are able to grow into seeds.

The Cucumber flowers are of two kinds, like those of the marrow. Perhaps now, you can guess why the gardener is careful to open his frames every day. He must not only let in the fresh air. He must also give the insects a chance to fly in to the flowers. For if they did not come, there would be no one to carry the pollen from one flower to the other. Some gardeners pick off a flower with dust-bags, and rub it against the sticky lumps of the large flower, and so do the same work as the insects.

Pumpkins, melons, and gourds have two kinds of flowers like the cucumber and marrow.

There is one more fruit which we eat as a vegetable, but I am not sure if you will have it in your garden. It is the beautiful tomato, which looks like a deep red apple. If you have not got it you should try to grow it. Cottagers often grow it in Devonshire, even when they have only a sandy path to plant it in.

Sow the seeds in a box in February, put a piece of glass over it, and keep it in the kitchen where it is warm. Then when the little plants have two or three leaves on them, put each plant in a small pot with some very sandy earth.

Keep the plants well watered, and in May put the pots outside the house in a warm corner. As soon as they are a little hardened you may scoop a deep hole in the bed, or path, under a sunny wall. Fill it with manure and earth, and put the plants in out of the pots. They will grow against the wall and give you fine tomatoes. Only you must be careful to keep off the slugs and snails, for they love the sweet tomato juice as much as we do.

When the fruits are big, if the weather is not warm enough for them to ripen out of doors, you may pick them and put them on the kitchen shelves and they will turn red and be fit to eat.

Bring the two kinds of flowers which grow on the vegetable marrow plant—also those of the cucumber. Bring in the fruit of a marrow, a cucumber, and a tomato.

LESSON VIII.

THE CABBAGE PLANT.

WHEN the spring flowers are beginning to peep out in the fields, your father will be hard at work in the garden. In March, if not before, neat seed beds of cabbage, broccoli, Brussels sprouts, and cauliflower will have to be sown, for planting out by-and-by. Early turnips must now be sown in their rows, and radishes and mustard and cress may be grown for salad.

All these belong to the family which have flowers in the form of a cross. So you see this is a very useful family to gardeners. It gives us, besides the lovely wallflower, the purple stock and the sweet alyssum in our flower garden, as well as the watercress in the brooks.

But as soon as our cabbage plants begin to grow, we find that the insects, which are so useful in helping to make seeds, can do harm in a kitchen garden. Early in May, before the

CABBAGE AND CABBAGE-BUTTERFLY.

plants are very large, you will see the white cabbage butterfly with two black spots on her wings, flitting about the garden.

Where do you think she has come from? All the winter her body has been covered with a hard gum, which spread over it when she wriggled out of her caterpillar skin, and fastened herself by silken threads to the stem of an old cabbage stalk, or hid perhaps in a crack in the palings.

Now that the sun is warm she has come out to lay her eggs. She does not feed on cabbages herself, she sips honey from the flowers. But she fed on leaves when she was a caterpillar, so she lays her eggs under a cabbage leaf, where the caterpillars will find food when they are hatched.

The Tortoiseshell Butterfly, out in the fields, lays her eggs on stinging nettles, because her caterpillars feed on nettle leaves. They weave a little tent under the leaves to come back to at night, and there you may find them.

But if you want to save your cabbages from being eaten by caterpillars, you must look for the eggs of the white cabbage butterfly under the cabbage leaves. They are very tiny, but in a fortnight they will hatch out into little green caterpillars with black spots, and a yellow line down their backs.

They eat and eat for about a month, and then about July or August they creep away to some tree or paling, and bind themselves there by their silken thread till next spring. Then each butterfly comes out to lay her eggs on fresh cabbages.

If you search very carefully all about your garden and in the shed, and along the palings in the winter, you may find and destroy the chrysalis and help to save your cabbages from the caterpillars.

But if you see some little white balls, about the size of a hemp-seed, lying near a dead caterpillar, take care not to destroy them. They are the cocoons of a little fly, which lays her egg in the body of the caterpillar of the white cabbage butterfly, and when the egg is hatched the grub feeds upon the inside of the caterpillar.

Is it not a curious history? The butterfly sucks honey from the flowers, and carries their pollen-dust for them. Then she lays her eggs under a cabbage leaf and dies. The caterpillar feeds on the cabbage, and then perhaps a little fly comes, and lays her egg in him; and the grub feeds on him, so that when the time comes for him to turn into a butterfly he dies instead.

Many other creatures feed on our cabbage. Slugs and snails like green meat and the gall weevil, which we saw feeding on the turnip, likes cabbage root as well. The best way to keep all enemies away is to make the ground clean and free from weeds, and to pick off all the insects you find.

Find any Crucifers (flowers formed in a cross) you can— wallflower, candytuft, stock, charlock, turnip, and any cabbage plant which is run to seed. Try to find the chrysalis of the cabbage butterfly.

LESSON IX.

HOW PLANTS DEFEND THEMSELVES.

In May the hedgerows will be full of flowers. I have not room to describe them all to you. You should pick one of each, on your way to school, and ask your teacher about them. On the tops of the banks, and nestling in the wood, you will find the wild hyacinths, which children call bluebells, and the red ragged-robin, and the lovely starworts or stitchworts with flowers like pure white stars and narrow pointed leaves. Children call these "snap-jacks," because the seed-box, when it is ripe, snaps if you pinch it. There are many kinds of starworts. One of them with small flowers is called chickweed.

The meadows are now golden with buttercups, and the ditches are blue with forget-me-nots, and you can find the little blue Speedwell or Bird's-eye almost anywhere. It is a weed, with thin weak stalks, and you may know it by its four blue petals, and its two stamens standing out like horns. Before long the tall Meadow-sweet, with its clusters of tiny white flowers, will be blooming by the side of the streams and in damp places; and the pretty little Bird's-foot Trefoil will brighten the hedgerows and fields.

You will know this little flower well. It grows quite low down, and is like a very small yellow pea-flower. About four or five little blossoms grow on the top of each flower-stalk, and the buds have bright red streaks upon them. When the pods are ripe they stand out like the toes of a bird's foot.

These, and many other flowers, you can find in the fields and hedges and you know now how to look for their seed-boxes and dust-bags; and I am sure you will watch to see what flies and bees and beetles come to fetch honey and pollen-dust.

If you do this and keep your eyes open, you will find out that other creatures come to the plants and flowers, which are not as useful to them as the bees. There is the cow, which takes large mouthfuls of their leaves as she grazes. There is the donkey, which feeds on the thistles. There is the rabbit, which comes out in the evening, to nibble at the tender young shoots;

and there are the little field-mice, which scrape away the earth and feed on the thick stems and roots underground.

Now let me tell you of a few plants which protect themselves, and perhaps you can find more. First come the Anemone and the meadow Buttercup. Both these have bitter leaves which burn your tongue when you bite them. If you walk across a field which has many buttercups in it you will find that the cows and the sheep have left them alone as much as they can. If they eat the leaves, they will not touch the flowers, which are much the most acrid. So these plants prevent the cows from killing them. In the same way the leaves of wild geraniums have a disagreeable taste and smell.

Then there are the Ferns. They have a great deal of bitter tannin in them. You will find that if cows or sheep have been feeding where the Bracken fern is growing, they will not have touched it. So the ferns keep themselves safe.

Then the little Wood-sorrel tastes acid, and the Speedwells dry up the inside of your mouth if you eat their leaves. So these plants are left alone. Lastly the Parson-in-the-pulpit has such poisonous berries, leaves, and underground stems, that no animal will eat it above ground, and no sensible field-mouse would think of nibbling at it underground.

Then there are the plants which grow thorns on their stems. Cows and horses do not like to eat gorse for it hurts their tender mouths. These are a few examples. I cannot give you more, because I want to tell you of something even more curious.

Plants want bees and flies to visit their flowers, because they carry their pollen from flower to flower. But other insects, such as ants and spiders, like honey too, and they only crawl; they

1. RAGGED ROBIN.   2. SUN-SPURGE.   3. TEASEL.

rub off any dust which falls on them before they reach another flower. So they rob the flowers of their honey and do nothing in return.

How do you think the plants protect themselves? In many different ways. The Teasel has a large flower-head full of honey. But the ants cannot steal it because its leaves grow opposite to each other on the stem, and join round it so that they make a little basin. The dew and the rain collect in the basin, and stop the ants from creeping past.

Then the plants we call Campions, of which the ragged-robin is one, often have their flower stems covered with fine hairs, and the stem near the flower is very sticky. When the ants climb up to try to steal the honey they stick fast, and can get no further. This is why some of the campions are often called "catch-flies."

A very common plant in the hedges is the Sun-spurge, which has curious small green flowers. This plant has a poisonous milky juice in its stem. When the ants try to climb up, they prick holes with their claws, and stick fast and die.

I wish I could tell you more of the way in which plants protect themselves by prickles, by hairs, and by poisons, but you must look for yourselves.

Bring in sun-spurge, campion or catch-fly, wood-sorrel, bracken, teasel, and wild geranium.

LESSON X.

WILD FLOWERS AND GARDEN FLOWERS.

Now you know how wild plants grow, how insects help to make the seeds, and how plants have to defend themselves from enemies which would eat their leaves or steal their honey.

Next let us look at the flowers in our gardens and see how far they are like the wild ones in the fields. All garden plants grow wild in some part of the world. We have taken them into our gardens, and made their flowers larger and brighter. Some still live wild in England, others have been brought from foreign countries.

The forget-me-nots in the garden border are very much the same as those we find in the lanes. The snowdrop has run wild in many parts of England. The lovely blue periwinkle, with its dark shiny leaves, grows in every Devonshire lane. The large ox-eye daisies which grow in our gardens are the same as those in the cornfields. The honey-suckle is as fine in the hedges as on the trellis-work of the porch.

But the large purple clematis and the beautiful yellow and white chrysanthemums, which grow in so many cottage gardens, come from abroad. I knew an old woman once who called them "Christmas anthems." I think she imagined that they flowered late in the year on purpose for Christmas.

The lovely yellow and purple pansies, which bloom all the summer, seem at first too grand to have come from wild ones. But you can gather small wild pansies in the lanes, and if you look inside the flower of the garden pansy you will see the curious bird's head on the top of its seed-box which we found in the violet. So the pansy, or Heartsease, is a true English plant.

I am sure you have some of the yellow and brown polyanthus in your garden. At first you will think there is nothing like it in the fields. But if you gather a cowslip and compare it with the polyanthus, you will find that all their parts are alike. For the polyanthus was once wild like the cowslip, and the gardeners have manured it, and chosen out the best seeds, till they have given it the bright colours it has now.

The reason that garden flowers are often larger and more beautiful in their colours than wild flowers is because the plants are not obliged to take so much pains to live nor to make so many seeds. The gardener puts them in good ground, feeds them well, and picks out the seeds of the best flowers to sow next year.

You can do the same if you try, and though you cannot do much in a few years you will get much finer flowers for your trouble. You must watch the plant and pick off all the withered leaves, and keep the ground raked, well manured, and free from weeds. Then you must settle which of the plants have the best and brightest flow-ers. Tie a little piece of cotton round the stem of these flowers, and watch when their seed-boxes are ripe, then keep these seeds to sow next year. In two or three years you will have much better flowers.

The pinks and carna-tions are some of the prettiest and sweetest of our garden flowers. They belong to an English family, called the Pink

WILD PANSY AND GARDEN PANSY.

Family. You may perhaps not have any wild pinks in your part of the country. But you will have the ragged robin and the campion, and these belong to the same family.

If you compare their flowers with the pink, you will find that they both have narrow leaves growing opposite each other. The stem is swollen at the joint where they grow. They both have a long green cup with points, and five pink or white petals, ragged at the edge. Ten stamens grow inside on the top of the stem, and there is a tall seed-box in the middle, with two or three sticky horns.

Now try to find a ripe seed-box. It will be open at the top and its points bend out like the top of a vase. Inside is a little upright pillar with the seeds growing round it. When you find all this in a flower you will know that it belongs to the Pink Family.

Chickweed, starwort, campion, soapwort, ragged robin, and wild pink can all be found in the lanes.

But no doubt you have in your garden some double flowers—pinks, wallflowers, stocks, and roses. These have a great many coloured petals, and hardly any dust-bags or seed-box, sometimes none at all. Gardeners have made these double flowers by growing the plants in very rich earth, and sowing the seeds of those which grew the most flower-leaves instead of stamens.

Plants in the fields hardly ever have double flowers. They must make plenty of seeds. If you turn a plant with double flowers out into poor ground and let it run wild, it will go back to single flowers. But gardeners want fine blooms. So they grow double hollyhocks, dahlias, peonies, and primroses, as well as single ones.

Compare wild and garden rose, wild and garden pansy, cowslip and polyanthus, pink and ragged robin.

WILD ROSE AND GARDEN ROSE.

LESSON XI.

THE ROSE FAMILY AND ITS FRUITS.

In June the, dog-roses are in bloom. They look very pretty thrusting their pink and white flowers out of the hedge. Though they have thorns, you can manage to cut a branch and take it to school. We will learn to-day about the rose family.

I shall want you to bring a good many flowers and fruits from the hedges and the garden, besides the rose. You remember that some of our best vegetables come from the flowers shaped like a cross. Now you will see that some of our best fruits come from the Rose Family.

So bring from the hedges a branch of wild rose. It must be wild, for you remember our garden roses have turned most of their stamens into flower leaves. Next get if you can a piece of bramble with a blackberry flower on it. Then from the bank below bring a wild strawberry plant. Get one if you can with a ripe strawberry hanging on it, as well as the flower. For there is another plant called the potentilla which is so like the wild strawberry that you might bring it by mistake, unless you saw the little strawberry fruit.

Then bring from your garden a strawberry, a raspberry, a cherry, and a plum, a green apple and a pear. What a number we shall have! And yet you might bring a peach, a medlar, a quince, a nectarine, and an apricot as well, for all these fruits belong to the Rose Family. Only I expect you will not have them in your garden.

First let us look at the flowers. You will see that the Wild Rose has a very deep cup, with five green sepals, which stick out in long points.

FRUITS OF THE ROSE FAMILY.

1. Haws of the Rose. *2.* Raspberry. *3.* Blackberry. *4.* Strawberry

If it is a dog-rose its crown will be made of five lovely pink petals. They are all separate, so that you can pull each one off the green cup, without disturbing the others. If you pull them all off, you will find that there are a great many dust-bags growing on the rim of the green cup.

Now look for the seed-boxes. Their sticky tops are peeping out of the cup. But you will have to tear the cup open to find them inside. Then you will see that they are all separate and that each one has a sticky top of its own.

Now look at the Strawberry flower: it too has five green sepals and five white petals, and a great many dust-bags, just like the rose. But it has no deep cup. Its seed-boxes grow on a little mound inside the sepals. By-and-by this mound will swell and grow soft and juicy and sweet, and the tiny seed-boxes will be buried in it, like pins in a pincushion. Look at the little fruit of the wild strawberry and the big fruit of the garden strawberry and you will see this. People often call these dry pips "seeds," but they are not seeds, they are tiny seed-boxes, each with one seed inside.

Now look at the Blackberry flower. It is just like the strawberry, and its seed-boxes grow on a mound. But when the fruit is ripe, you will find that the mound is no bigger. In the blackberry, the seed-boxes themselves grow soft, and become small balls full of sweet juice. You can separate them one from another, and you will find a seed inside each.

The Raspberry is like the blackberry, only the little red juicy seed-boxes shrink away from the mound. So you can pull them off like a cap, leaving the white pointed mound behind.

And now how about the other fruits? Next spring when the

Plum trees and Cherry trees are in bloom, you will find that they have the same kind of flowers as the rose. But they have only one seed-box to each flower. This seed-box grows juicy outside, and leaves a very hard shell inside, round the seed. So you have to eat the juicy covering and crack the hard shell before you can get at the kernel or seed.

The Apple and the Pear will puzzle you, till you cut an apple across. Then you will see the five little seed-boxes arranged like a star in the middle of the fruit. Each seed-box will have one or two pips or seeds in it, and the boxes are what we call the core of the apple. The green cup has grown thick and fleshy all round them. You can see the dried tips of the

1. BLACKBERRY FLOWER.
   Cut across, showing separate Fruits.

2. CHERRY FLOWER.
   Showing the Single Fruit and Fruit.

3. APPLE.
   Cut across, showing the five Seed-boxes.

green sepals on the top of the apple. In the apple blossom the seed-boxes are separate, till the cup grows round them, and makes one big apple.

Bring a wild rose, a piece of blackberry in flower, a wild strawberry in flower, an apple, pear, plum, cherry, raspberry and garden strawberry.

LESSON XII.

THE DEAD-NETTLE AND THE PEA-FLOWER.

WHEN a bee goes in search of honey, there is one plant she is very glad to find. This is the Dead-nettle. She does not mind whether it has white or purple flowers. She knows that unless some other bee has been there before her she will find some honey.

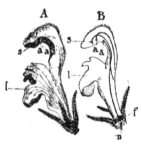

A. FLOWER OF THE
DEAD-NETTLE.

B. FLOWER CUT IN
HALF.

a. Anthers.   *s*. Stigma.
f. Fringe of Hairs.
n. Fruit or Seed-boxes.
l. Lip.

There are generally plenty of dead-nettles to be found, for their leaves do not taste nice, and they look so like stinging-nettles that very few animals will eat them.

The real nettle has only small green flowers, while the dead-nettle has clusters of red or white blossoms growing all round the stem, just above each pair of leaves. These flowers are shaped like helmets, and they have a broad lip hanging down in front, which has a deep notch in the middle.

The stem of the plant is not round, like the stems of most plants. It is square with four sides. By this you may always know it from a stinging-nettle, even when it is not in flower. The coarse leaves grow opposite to each other, and each pair grows across the one below it, as we saw in Lesson II.

Now let us look at the flower. You had better take a white dead-nettle, as the flowers are large. Take hold of the helmet and pull it very gently. It will come off, leaving the green cup with its five points. But most likely you will have brought away the long tube with sticky horns, which grows out of the seed-box, for it comes off very easily.

If you have, try another flower, and tear the helmet open very carefully. Then you will see that at the bottom of the cup there are four little seed-boxes, like nuts, with a long tube standing right up in the middle of them. It has two sticky horns.

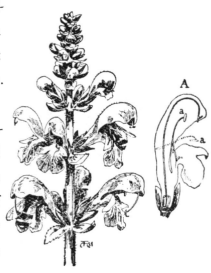

Now look inside another flower. You will find four stamens growing on the crown, and two of them are so long that they reach right up into the hood. Before you pulled the hood off the sticky horns were close to them. At the bottom of

BEES IN MEADOW-SAGE.

A. Flower cut open to show how the Anther (*a*) swings as the Bee goes in.

the tube there is plenty of honey, but creeping insects cannot get it, for there is a thick fringe of hairs in the tube to keep them away.

But when the bee comes for honey, she pushes her trunk through the hairs, and as she sucks she brushes the dust out of the bags. Then she goes to another flower and leaves it on the sticky horns. There are a great many flowers with lips like the dead-nettle. Mint, Sage, Balm, Thyme, Peppermint, Lavender, Rosemary, and the pretty blue and white bugle flowers in the hedges are all lipped—you will know them by their square stems, opposite leaves, and the four little seed-boxes.

In Sage plants the anthers swing on a bar. The bee hits her head against the lower end, which is empty, and the full dust-bag comes down on her back.

Another flower which the bee loves is the Pea. There again

she is sure to find honey. In the kitchen garden on a fine morning you will see the bees buzzing along the rows of peas and beans, and only stopping to poke their heads into the flowers.

PEA-FLOWER AND SECTION.
a. Anthers. *b.* Sticky beak.
o. Ovary. *s.* Seeds.

Get a pea-flower and let us see how they do it. Hold the flower facing you. At the back is one large petal, with a deep dent in the middle. This stands up like a flag to tell the bee where to come for honey. So it is called the "standard." Two smaller petals are folded together, just below it. These are called "wings." Between these wings are two more petals, which are joined together like the end of a boat. These are called the "keel."

If you take hold of the wings, and pull them gently down, you will find they bring the keel with them. Then you will see the dust-bags of ten stamens and the sticky beak of the tiny pea-pod. These were hidden before in the keel.

If you pick the flower to pieces, you will see why the keel came down. Inside each wing there is a knob, which fits into a hollow in the side of the keel. Is not this curious? When the bee settles on the wings, she presses them down with her weight. They press down the keel, and the dust-bags knock against the breast of the bee. So she goes away to the next flower covered with pollen-dust.

There are almost as many flowers like the pea as there are like the dead-nettle. The beautiful yellow Gorse, the little Trefoil, and all the Vetches in the hedges belong to this family. So do the sweet Clovers which we grow for clover hay. Each head of clover is a cluster of tiny flowers shaped like a pea.

Then in the flower garden we have the Laburnum, and in the kitchen garden the Scarlet-runners and the Broad Beans.

Examine a dead-nettle, mint, thyme, and meadow-sage. Notice the curious swinging anther of the meadow-sage. Also a pea blossom, gorse blossom, tare, and bird's-foot trefoil.

LESSON XIII.
CLIMBING PLANTS.

WHEN you were picking the flowers of the peas and scarlet-runners, if you kept your eyes open, you must have noticed that they climb up the sticks which we put for them. But I daresay you did not ask yourself why they climb, nor how they climb.

You know that if you took the sticks away they would fall in a tangled mass on the ground. For peas and scarlet-runners have thin weak stems. They could not get enough light and air all tumbled together on the ground. They would be stifled under other plants. So they have learnt to climb up on a hedge or sticks, or anything they can find, to lift them towards the sky.

That is why they climb, now let us see how they do it. For they do not both set to work in the same way.

You will find on the pea-plant that in many places where a leaf ought to be, there is a little curled green thread, which clings round the twig of the stick, just as a baby clings to its mother's finger. We call these threads "tendrils." They hold the plant up to the light and air, and let the blossoms hang out where the bees can find them. The scarlet-runners do their climbing differently. They do not use their leaves, but twine their whole stem round the sticks.

PEA CLIMBING BY TENDRILS.

If you look along the hedges you will find many climbing plants, which manage to use the thick bushes as a sort of bank on which to spread out their leaves and flowers. There is the Clematis, or Traveller's Joy. It has not turned its leaves into tendrils, nor twined its stem. It twists the stalk of the leaves tightly round the twigs, so that the leaves stand out at the end. Its pretty greenish flowers are spread in this way all over the top of the hedge, and by-and-by the feathery seed-boxes will hang like an old man's beard, just where the wind can catch them to blow them away.

I think you must know the Goose-grass or Cleavers, which grows over everything in the lanes. Its narrow green leaves are

HONEYSUCKLE TWINING ROUND A STEM.

arranged round the stem like a star, and it has very tiny white flowers. The stem, leaves and seed-boxes are all crowded with tiny hooks so that it clings to your hand when you gather it. It is really a very weak plant, but it clings to other plants which are stronger, and so raises itself up.

The blackberry and other brambles climb in the same way, and the wild rose climbs by its thorns. Further along the hedgerow the wild Hop may be growing. Its stems die down every year and grow up again in the spring. Yet it manages to

1. WILD CLEMATIS OR TRAVELERS JOY.
2. GARDEN PURPLE CLEMATIS.

spread a long way, for its stem twines round twigs and small trees, and everything it can find, spreading out its broad leaves shaped like a heart. You will find the flowers of the hop rather puzzling, for its dust-bags and seed-boxes grow on different plants.

The Honeysuckle, too, twines its stem, as you must have seen on the porch or the paling. Sometimes when it twines round a young branch, it winds itself so tightly that the branch cannot grow in the places where the honeysuckle binds it. So it is marked all the way up, as if it had a ribbon round it.

Then there are the pretty plants called Tares or vetches, which have flowers like small pea-flowers. They climb everywhere by their tendrils. I think you will be able to find all these as well as the Convolvulus or bindweed, which twines round all plants, even our gooseberry and currant

GOOSE-GRASS.

bushes, and wants weeding out very carefully. But I am not quite sure whether you can find a curious plant called the Dodder. You must look for it on the common, climbing over the heath and gorse bushes. It is only a thin wiry stem, with clusters of tiny pink flowers on it. It has no leaves at all. How then can it live since it has no leaves to make food? It twines round the gorse, or heath, or clover, and sends its roots into their stems and sucks out ready-made food!

The Vine and the pretty Virginia creepers turn their small branches into threads for climbing. Very likely you have a Virginia creeper on your wall, which turns red in the autumn. Two kinds of this creeper have a very curious plan for climbing. When the threads, or tendrils, touch the wall, their tips turn red, and swell into little cushions. These cushions stick so fast to the wall that even when the branch is dead you have to pull them off. Lastly the Ivy climbs by small roots, which grow all along the stems.

Now you know all the four dodges which plants have for climbing. By hooks, by threads, by their roots, and by the whole plant twining itself round. Try to see how many you can find.

Bring one of each kind of climbing plant.

LESSON XIV.
HOW PLANTS STORE FOOD.

SOME plants live for one year only. Some live for two years. Some live for many years.

Have you not noticed that you have to sow mignonette, marigolds, and peas and beans fresh every year in the garden? —unless you keep the young seedlings, which grow from the seeds that fall. In the fields, wheat and oats only live till their grains are ripe, and then die away if they are left in the ground till winter comes.

In the same way chickweed, the corn poppy, and our old friend the shepherd's purse die when their seeds are ripe. These plants are like people who earn just enough to live from day to day, and cannot save for next year.

But if you want to have Sweet Williams, or Canterbury Bells in flower in the summer, you must sow the seeds the summer before. For these plants do not flower the first year. They only grow their root, and a short stem with leaves on it. The plant is busy making food, and storing it up in the root and stem, as starch and sugar and gum, so that it is ready to make a strong flowering plant next year.

Then after they have flowered and made their seeds, these plants die. They have only stored enough for a short life, and cannot live another year. Foxgloves, Thistles, and Wild Parsley behave in this way.

Lastly, you know that Snowdrops, Crocuses, Daisies, Primroses, Pansies, and Dahlias live on for many years, dying down in the autumn and coming up again in the spring. These plants send down the starch and sugar into the root, or the lower part of the stem, or into the bottom of the leaves underground.

Some of them grow more than two years before they try to flower. They are like people who save when they are young, and always go on saving, so that they have something to spare.

You can sometimes make a plant store up food. If you sow some mignonette and put one plant in a pot, and keep on nipping off the flower-buds so that it cannot make seeds, it will grow into a little shrub, and flower for two or three years.

Different plants store their food in different parts. The wild carrot and the acorn, which is growing into an oak, store theirs in the root. The carrot is fleshy and only lasts two years. But the root of the oak is woody and lives long.

The lesser celandine, you remember, stores its food in small white lumps like white sugar-plums, which are swollen roots with a bud at the top. The marsh marigolds, and the pretty yellow flags, which grow by the river, store theirs in an underground stem. You must follow the stalks of the marsh marigold right back till you come close to the roots, and there you will find the thick knob, which lives on, all through the winter, and sends up fresh leaves in the spring.

If you can get a long piece of the creeping stem of the yellow flag, you will see the marks of the places where the flowering stems have come up year after year. They follow each other along the stem till you come to the plant of this year. And beyond that is the bud for next year.

There is a very pretty plant called Solomon's Seal, which is wild in some parts of England, and is often grown in cottage gardens. It has a tall flower-stalk with rather narrow leaves, and lovely white flowers, with green tips, The flowers hang down all on one side of the stalk. If you dig up a piece of the stem of this plant you will see large scars like seals upon it. These are the places where the stems have grown year after year, and this is why it is called Solomon's Seal.

You can make out for yourself the mass of stems and buds people call a primrose root. I want now to show you an underground bud or bulb. Dig up a wild hyacinth, usually called a blue-bell. You will find that it has a large knob at the bottom, with small roots growing out of it. Cut this knob in half, and notice that it is a bulb made of scaly leaves folded one over the other, exactly like an onion.

If you dig it up in the spring, the flower-stalk will be standing up in the middle, and when you pull the scaly leaves off one by one, you will find another bud very small close to the bottom of the flower-stalk. If you dig up another plant in the autumn, the flower-stalk will have withered away, and the baby bud will be peeping out of the top of the bulb.

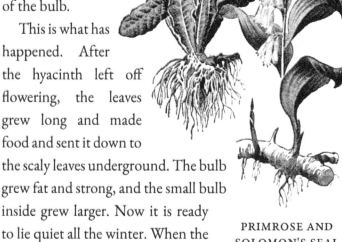

This is what has happened. After the hyacinth left off flowering, the leaves grew long and made food and sent it down to the scaly leaves underground. The bulb grew fat and strong, and the small bulb inside grew larger. Now it is ready to lie quiet all the winter. When the spring comes the little bulb will take

PRIMROSE AND
SOLOMON'S SEAL.

the food from the thick scaly leaves, and grow into a new plant.

Bring six plants—two with food stored in the root, two in the underground stem, two in bulbs.

LESSON XV.

UNDERGROUND VEGETABLES.

Now you will be able to understand how it is that we get such nourishing vegetables from the kitchen garden. The bees take honey and pollen from the flowers of plants. We take the sugar and starch and other food, which they store up in their leaves, and stems, and roots.

Carrots, Parsnips, and Beet-roots are plants which store up food in their roots the first year, and flower the second year. So we sow them, and feed them very well the first year, and when they have laid up a good store of sweet food, we pull them up and eat them before they can flower.

If you can get your father to leave one of these plants in the ground till the second year, you will see it flower and make its seeds. But a turnip will flower in the first year, if you sow it early in the spring, and leave it all the summer. This is why we sow our largest stock of turnips in June and July so that they may not flower before we want them in the winter.

Now I think I hear a little boy saying, "She has forgotten potatoes." No, I have not. But potatoes are not roots, like carrots and turnips. Cut one open and you will see some dark spots in it called "eyes." Indeed you may see them without cutting if you wash it and look carefully.

Each of these eyes is a little bud, with a growing tip, and the beginning of leaves. Now you know that a root cannot bear leaves. It can only have one bud on the top where the stem begins. So the Potato cannot be a root.

Neat time you dig up some potatoes for dinner, look at the roots carefully before you shake off the potatoes. You will then

UNDERGROUND VEGETABLES.

A carrot badly-grown and well-grown. Asparagus in the bud, as we eat it, and with its red seeds as it ripens. Onion cut across to show the scaly leaves in which food is stored.

see that each potato grows at the end of a white stalk, very different from the roots. For a potato is a swelling at the end of a stem, which grows underground. It is a "tuber" like the Jerusalem Artichokes, which I expect you also have in the garden.

If you cut up either an artichoke or a potato into pieces, and leave a bud in each piece, it will grow up into a new plant, and send down food into the stems below the ground, and form more tubers. The potato plant flowers, and forms seed every year. The seed-box is poisonous, and so are the seedboxes of many of the Potato Family. The Deadly Nightshade, with its dark black berries, belongs to this family. It is never safe to eat any berry, or other fruit, unless you know what it is, for many berries which even the birds eat, are poisonous to some animals and to man.

The potato plant stores its poison only in its seed-box, which is green, there is none in the potato. The potato disease which gives us so much trouble is a little plant like the mould on jam, which eats the potato away.

In Celery we eat the stems which grow above ground. But we earth them up to keep them white. For plants cannot become green without sunlight. In Asparagus we eat the green stem with the bud at the top. Those buds which we do not eat branch out in summer, and have beautiful leaves and bright red berries.

Lastly in Onions, Leeks, and Shallots we eat the bulbs, or underground buds, like that of the hyacinth. They have plenty of good food in them stored up in the scaly leaves.

Now let us see what you must do if you want your roots,

bulbs, and stems to grow into good vegetables. First you must drain the ground if it wants it, and dig it deeply and break the earth up so that the roots have no hard lumps in their way and can grow straight and strong. Then you must dig in some manure. And be careful that you dig it in deep, for grubs and maggots like carrots and onions as much as we do; and in the autumn and spring, when you dig the garden, they are lying about in their cocoon shells. If you bury them deeply in the ground, then when they turn into flies they cannot get out to lay eggs.

There is another way in which you can get the better of them. Each plant has its own grub which feeds upon it. There is the grub of the onion fly, of the carrot fly, and so on. So when you sow your seed, if you sow the carrots where the onions were last year, and the onions in the old parsnip bed, when the fly is hatched she does not find the leaves for her eggs close at hand, and you may save your roots.

Then in such plants as carrots and onions you must keep the roots and bulbs well covered, and when you thin them out you must make the ground firm again. For the onion fly and the carrot fly lay their eggs on the root or bulk), and if they cannot find their way in, the root is safe.

Lastly, you know the troublesome wireworm which wriggles along just underground and eats everything it finds. To be even with him you must keep the ground clean, for he likes rubbish to hide in, and you had better mix some salt or lime with the earth. If he is still troublesome you can put some slices of potato just under the ground and stick a twig in, to show where they are, and you are pretty sure to find him underneath in the early morning.

Bring six vegetables—1. root; 2. bulb; 3. stem; 4. tuber; 5. leaves; 6, flowers.

LESSON XVI.

HOW SEEDS TRAVEL

In the autumn, when the plants have left off flowering, there is plenty for us to do in looking for fruits, and finding out how they scatter their seeds.

Some drop them near at home. The poppy, as we saw, has a hard fruit with little openings under the cover. When the stalk bends the seeds fall out through these holes and grow in the ground all around.

If you look at the dry seed-boxes of the wild geranium which grows in the lanes, you will see that each one has curled up from the bottom. There will be five little curls round the sticky knob in the middle, and the seeds will be gone.

There is a tall yellow Balsam which is found wild in some parts of England, and another with reddish flowers, which is often grown in cottage gardens, which have a most amusing seed-box. When it is ripe it bursts open and flings out its seeds. If you can get a friend to touch a ripe pod, it will make you laugh to see how he jumps as it pops with a bang in his hand. This is why the plant is often called "touch-me-not."

But plants want their seeds to be carried farther away than even popping will send them. Think how many flowers there are crowded together in a hedgerow. If all the seeds fell close

1. BURDOCK.
2. WILD GERANIUM, WITH SEED-BOXES (S) CURLED UP.

round they would stifle each other. So plants try all sorts of plans to get their seeds scattered.

I am sure you have blown the feathery dandelion "clocks" on your way home from school. Next time you do it look at one of the little floating messengers. Do you remember that when we looked at the dandelion we found that it was a flower-head with hundreds of tiny flowers, and that each flower had an oval seed-bag at the bottom with a number of fine hairs on the top of it and a yellow crown with a long strap?

Now the yellow crown has withered away, and the top of the seed-box his grown up into a long neck with the hairy sepals on the top. And when the wind catches these hairs it carries the tiny fruit along perhaps for miles, and then it drops down to grow.

Thistles and sow-thistles, groundsel and teasels, and a number of other flowers of that kind have these feathery seeds. So you see when you let them grow on your own ground you spoil the ground of other people as well.

This is the way that wind carries seeds.

Other seeds are washed down by streams and left on their banks. Others, again, are often carried in the mud that sticks to the feet of birds.

Another plan is to grow tiny hooks on the seed-boxes so that animals carry them. The goose-grass does this. We saw that it has tiny hooks all over its stem and leaves, which it uses for climbing. It has the same kind of hooks on its tiny seeds. If you take a bunch of goose-grass in your hand you will get a number of the very small seed-boxes sticking to your fingers.

But there is a much bigger "burr," which grows on the common Burdock in the lanes. The burdock is a tall plant, with very large heart-shaped leaves and pink flower-heads, something like a thistle. You often bring its burrs home on your clothes, dogs carry them in their hair, and sheep in their fleece. Each of these burrs is a cup of leaves covered with hooks. The leaves grow together into a ball with the flowers peeping out at the top, and if you open a ripe burr you will find the tiny fruit inside.

So you, and the dogs, and the sheep carry the seeds for the plants.

But the prettiest plan of all is when the seed-box grows into a sloe, or a cherry, or into some bright berry like the berries of the hawthorn and the honeysuckle. For then the birds come to eat the nice fruit, and when they carry it off to some tree near they drop the stone down in a new place. Or they eat the berry, and the hard seeds pass through their body, and fall with their droppings somewhere far off.

Now you see why the blackberry and the raspberry grow juicy pulp round their seeds, and why the little hard seed-boxes of the strawberry stick in the juicy mound. All this is to tempt the birds to eat them and carry their seeds.

So too in the hip of the wild rose, the green cup grows large and soft, and turns a bright red just when winter is coming, and there is not much food. Then the birds come and peck at the cup, and the seed-boxes inside stick to their beaks or are swallowed, and so are carried away.

You know that in a hard winter the holly berries and mistletoe, the hips and haws, and even the berries of the yew and the honeysuckle, are often all gone before Christmas. But I daresay you did not know before that the birds were carrying about seeds to grow up next year.

But if you keep your eyes open, you can learn a great many things like these, which children shut up in towns cannot see. You are happy to live in the beautiful country, among the birds and the flowers. You breathe the fresh air, which the plants make sweet, you gather your own flowers, and grow your own vegetables and fruit, and you can watch the plants in your garden growing prettier every year.

Try to find the fruits of the wild geranium, yellow balsam, dandelion, groundsel, thistle, teasel, goose-grass, burdock, rose, hawthorn, honeysuckle, yew, and other plants.

BOOK IV
BIRDS OF THE AIR

"EYES AND NO EYES"

---

fourth Book.

BIRDS OF THE AIR.

LESSON I.
BIRDS WE KNOW.

I WONDER how many birds you know by sight, and what you could tell about their nests and their lives?

There are between three and four hundred different British birds, and very few people know them all. But in any one place there are not more common birds than you could learn in a year. You can look for the rare ones afterwards.

The best way to begin is to write down those you are sure about, and say how you recognise them. You cannot mistake a Robin, with his red breast, his plump little body, and his brown wings. The mother robin's breast is not quite so red, and the young have no red at all. But when you have seen them with the cock-robin, you will soon know them by their shape.

But a Chaffinch has a red breast. How can you tell him from a robin? His breast is much browner than the robin's, and even at a distance you may know him by the white bands on his dark wings, and the yellow tips to some of his feathers. Then his body is longer, and he moves more gracefully than the robin, while his loud "pink, pink," if you go near his nest, will tell you at once what he is.

The Lark you know by his slender brown body and white speckled throat, and by the way he soars, as he sings his sweet song. The common green Woodpecker is easily known by his bright colours, his curious feet, and his stiff tail, which he uses to jerk himself up a tree. And though a Nuthatch also goes up a tree by jumps, you would never take him for a woodpecker, for he is no bigger than a sparrow, and he has a short tail and blue-grey wings and a dingy red breast.

Then you know the cooing Wood-pigeon, the chattering Magpie, the soaring Hawk and his hooked beak, and the downy Owl. And I daresay you could tell me of many more.

The birds you know best will most of them be with us all the year round. But not all. The Swifts fly away to the south in August, and the Swallows and the Martins follow in October. When they are gone the Fieldfares come from the north, and feed in flocks on the worms in the damp fields, and on the holly berries when the ground is hard with frost.

The Swallow and the House Martin are so alike that, as they come and go together, you might not know them apart, unless you remember that a Swallow has a blue-black collar across his breast, and that the fork of his tail is longer than that of the Martin. You may be busy all the year round watching the birds, seeing when they come and go, what food they eat, how they fly, whether they sing in the morning or evening, and where they build their nests.

Many farmers and gardeners shoot little birds because they eat their corn and peas and fruit. But a large number of birds feed chiefly on insects. You ought to know which these are, for they are very useful in clearing away earwigs and caterpillars, as well as slugs and snails. If you look out early some morning and see a Thrush tapping a snail-shell against a stone to get at the snail, you will say he is a good gardener. You will not grudge him a little fruit in the summer.

Then there are the nests and the young birds to watch. You need not take the nests, nor rob the birds of their eggs. You will learn much more by pulling back the leaves and the twigs, and peeping gently into the nest. For then you can come another day and watch when the eggs hatch, and how the young birds grow. If you are careful not to disturb the bush nor touch the eggs, the mother will not desert them. Last year a pair of Thrushes built their nest in a hedge by the side of a path where people were always passing. But though I went often to look at it, the mother brought up all her four little ones. She would even sit still on the nest when I peeped in, while her mate sang on a tree close by.

Point out and describe six birds common in the neighbourhood.

LESSON II.
THE SONG OF BIRDS.

BIRDS sing when they are happy, and cry out when they are frightened, just as children do. Only they have songs and cries of their own. You can always tell when the little song-birds are happy, for each one trills out his joyous notes as he sits on a branch of a tree, or the top of a hedge.

In the early morning of the spring, you will hear singing in

the garden almost before it is light. First there is a little chirping and twittering, as if the birds were saying "good-morning"
and preparing their throats. Then, as the sun rises, there comes
a burst of song.

Robins, Thrushes, Blackbirds, Chaffinches, and Wrens
whistle away merrily, and many other little birds join in. While
they are all singing together, it is not easy to tell one song from
another, though the Thrush sings loudest and clearest of all.

Then they fly away to their breakfast and, as the day goes
on, you hear one or two at a time. So you can listen to the notes
of each song, and if you go near very quietly, you can see the
throat of the bird swelling and quivering as he works the little
voice-chords inside, which make the notes.

It is not easy to write down what a bird sings, for it is like
whistling—there are no words in it. But people often try to
imitate their songs in words. Listen to the Thrush. You can
fancy he says "cherry-tree, cherry-tree, cherry-tree" three times.
Then, after some other notes, he sings "hurry-up, hurry-up,"
and "go-it, go-it." For the thrush has a great many notes.

The pretty Yellowhammer, with its bright yellow head,
sings "a little bit of bread, and no che-e-s-e." The Chiff-chaff
calls "chiff-chaff, chiff-chaff" quite distinctly. Any child can
imitate the cuckoo, or the coo-oo-oo of the wood-pigeon.

As the days grow hotter, the birds sing less. They sit on the
branches of the trees, or on the hedges under the shade of the
leaves, or hop about in the wood.

Then when the evening comes, and long shadows creep
over the grass, each bird looks out for his supper. When he is

satisfied he sings his evening song of content, before he goes to sleep.

What a concert it is! Finches, tomtits, sparrows, wrens, robins, and chaffinches all singing at once. And above them all, come the song of the thrushes and blackbirds, the cooing of the wood-pigeon and the caw-caw of the rooks as they fly home from the fields. As the thrushes were the first to begin in the morning, except the lark, so they are the last to leave off at night, and often one thrush will go on long after all the others are quiet.

Then at last all seem to have settled down for the night. But no! If you live in Kent, or any part of the south or east of England, you may hear in May or June a sweet sound, like a flute, coming softly from many parts of the wood. This comes from the Nightingales, who, in the warm summer, will sing nearly all night.

They sing in the day as well, but their note is so soft that often you cannot hear it when more noisy birds are singing. In the still night you can hear the sweet song rising up six notes and then bubbling like a flute played in water. When you have once heard a nightingale sing you will never forget it. In Yorkshire or Devonshire you will not hear him, for he does not go so far to the North or to the West.

Birds sing most in the spring, for then they are making their nests, and the father bird sings to the mother while she is building, and when she is sitting on the eggs. You may often find out where a Robin's nest is hidden by seeing the cock-robin sitting on a branch singing to his mate. Most people too, have seen the Wood-pigeon puffing out his throat and cooing and bowing to the mother bird on her nest. For pigeons make love all the year round.

When the mother bird is sitting, the father bird sings for joy, and when the young birds are hatched he teaches them his song. Song-birds have very delicate throats. They have muscles, which quiver like the strings of a violin, and the young birds have to learn to work these muscles.

It is curious to hear a young Blackbird or Thrush beginning to try a tune. First he sounds one note, then two or three. They are not always in tune, but he tries again and again. So little by little he learns his father's song.

Listen to the song of birds—robins, thrushes, blackbirds, larks, nightingales, bullfinches and others, and try to imitate them by whistling.

LESSON III.

THE NESTS OF BIRDS.

IF you want to know how cleverly nests are made, you should collect a few which the birds have deserted, or from which the young birds have flown.

You will find a Hedge-sparrow's nest in many a hawthorn bush, and though it is a simple nest, I think you will find, if you pull it to pieces, that you cannot put it together again as well as the bird did.

A Chaffinch's nest is more finely woven. You will most likely find one in the apple trees in the orchard. It is made of dry grass and moss matted together with wool in the shape of a deep cup, and lined with hair and feathers. Outside, the bird will most likely have stuck pieces of grey or white lichen.

THRUSHES AND NEST.

Lichen is the papery-looking plant which grows on apple trees, and which children call grey moss. The pieces woven in help to hide the nest in an apple tree. When the Chaffinch builds in a green hedge she often uses green moss instead.

Now try to find a Thrush's nest. It may be in a laurel-bush or a fir-tree. It is large and quite firm, not soft like the hedge-sparrows nest. For the thrush plasters the inside with mud, or cow-dung, or rotten wood, till it is almost as hard as the inside of a cocoa-nut shell.

When you have looked at these nests, you will want to see one built next spring. But this is not so easy. For birds try to hide the cradles of their little ones, and do not like to work when anyone is near.

Rooks are the easiest to watch, for they build in high trees, and therefore are not shy. You may see them flying along with pieces of stick in their mouths, and bringing mud and clay to plaster them together. Sometimes you may see the old rooks staying behind in the rookery, to steal the sticks from the nests of the young rooks while they are away, instead of fetching them for themselves.

Birds do not all make the same shaped nests. The Lark makes her nest of grass in a rut or a furrow of the field. The green Plover or Peewit, whose cry you know so well, "pee-weet, pee-weet," lays a few bits of grass, or rush, in a marsh or in a rough field. Her little ones run about as soon as they come out of the egg.

The Swallows build their nests of mud and straw on the rafters of barns, or under the ledges of chimneys, in the shape of a shallow basin, and line them with feathers. But the Martins build under the eaves. They make their nests of clay stuck against the wall like a bag, with only a small hole at the top. It is very funny to see the tail of a martin sticking out, when she puts her head into her nest to feed the young ones.

The Woodpecker makes a hole in a tree for her nest, and lines it with chips of wood. The Nuthatch looks out for a hole in a branch, and lines it with flakes of bark and dry leaves. Then, if it is too big, she fills up the opening with clay, all except one little hole.

Rooks and Pigeons build coarse nests. The rooks build theirs of sticks and turf lined with grass and moss. The pigeon leaves hers so loose that the eggs almost slip through.

Then the little singing birds, the Warblers, the Thrushes, the Nightingales, and the Robins build lovely cup-nests. Reed-warblers weave their nest round two

REED-WARBLERS' NEST. or three reeds, or other plants, near the water. It is made of blades of grass and lined with water-weed. The Wren, the long-tailed Titmouse, and the Chiff-chaff, build nests in the shape of a ball, with a hole in one side. The chiff-chaff lines hers with a

Wrens build in all sorts of strange places, in walls and trees, in holes of rocks, on the tops of hedges and on the banks of rivers. If you look about near the nest in which the wren has laid her eggs you will often find one or two other nests built exactly like it, but not lined with feathers. They are called "cock's nests." We do not know why the birds build them. Perhaps one day you may find out if you watch. The chiff-chaff hides her nests in the hedges or banks, and the long-tailed titmouse loves to build in the gorse bushes.

Once two Wrens were watched building their nest in a juniper tree. They began at seven o'clock in the morning. The mother wren brought some leaves from a lime-tree. She put one leaf in a fork of the tree, and laid the others round it. Then she went back for more. So she went on all day, bringing in leaves, and matting them together with moss, and all the while the cock-wren sang to her from the top of the tree.

By seven o'clock in the evening she had made the outside of the nest, in the shape of a ball with a hole in one side.

Next day the two birds began work together at half-past three in the morning. They worked for eight days, carrying in moss and feathers. When they had done, the nest was a firm little ball, lined with a thick layer of soft feathers, for the wee wrens to lie in, when they were hatched.

Then the mother wren laid five small white eggs with a few red spots upon them, and sat for a whole fortnight, while her mate sang to her, and brought her insects to eat.

EXAMINE NESTS. *Mud-built*—swallow, martin. *Roughly woven*—house-sparrow. *Cup-nests*—hedge-sparrow, chaffinch. *Woven and mud-lined*—thrush.

COCK AND HEN CHAFFINCH WITH THEIR NEST.

LESSON IV.

BIRDS' EGGS.

WHEN you have looked at several birds' nests, you will want to see what the eggs are like. Try first to find those which are near your home. Some are so well hidden, that you will have to watch where the old birds go in and out, before you can find them. Others, like the nests of rooks, magpies and jays, are easy to see, but not easy to reach.

Do not take the eggs. Each will hatch out into a happy little bird, and if you carried the egg home it would only be broken. Your teacher will very likely collect one of each kind, which will do to show the class for many years.

But look well at the eggs in the nest. Then you will know them again when you find them in another place. Count how many there are, and notice if any more are laid afterwards. Then reckon how long the eggs are being hatched, after the last one is laid. You will find it is about a fortnight for the small birds and a day or two longer for rooks and pigeons. Then you can watch the feeding of the young birds, which we shall talk about in the next two lessons.

It is better not even to touch the eggs; for some birds, like the wood-pigeon, will desert their nests if the eggs have been handled. Other birds are not so particular. Mr. Kearton tells us that when he was a boy he used to find plovers' nests and amuse himself by turning the large end of the egg into the middle of the nest. As soon as the tidy mother came back, she always turned them round again with the points in the middle. The baby bird always comes out at the large end, so this gives them more room, as they hatch out.

If you have a laurel hedge in the garden you may find a Thrush's nest in it, with four to six beautiful blue eggs, about an inch long and spotted with black at the large end. The mother will scold you well, and perhaps will not leave the nest, and you will have to take your chance when she is away. You may find a Blackbird's nest not far off. You will know it from the thrush's nest because it is lined with fine roots and grass, so is not hard inside. The eggs are greener with red-brown spots. The Misselthrush generally builds in a tree, and her eggs are a light buff colour spotted with reddish brown and pale lilac.

The Chaffinch will build close to your house, or in the apple trees of the orchard; and a pair of Bullfinches may make their nest in the ivy of the old garden wall, though they are shy birds. The chaffinch's eggs are a pale brown-green colour with brown spots. They are about one-third the size of the thrush's egg. The bullfinch's are a pale blue, spotted with brown or purple. Be careful when you look at the bullfinch's nest, for though the mother will sit still, the father will be angry, and he may make her desert her nest, if he sees you.

You will have to get a ladder if you want to see a Martin's nest, for they build under the eaves of the house. And when you pull away a little of the nest and look in, make sure that you see the right eggs, for a sparrow will often take a martin's nest and lay her eggs in it. You can find out, by watching which bird goes into the nest. But if you cannot do this, you may know by the colour of the eggs. A martin's egg is white without any spots upon it. A sparrow's egg is grey with brown blotches on it. When the sparrow builds her own nest, it is made of straw or hay lined with feathers. It has about five or six eggs in it.

It is easier to look into a Swallow's nest than into a martin's, for it is not covered at the top, and is often put upon a rafter in a barn. It will have about five white eggs in it, with dark red patches on them. Watch these nests carefully, for when the eggs are hatched it is very pretty to see the old swallows teaching the young ones to catch flies.

We must not forget the Robins, though I expect you know their eggs well. They are white, spotted with light red, and you may easily find them, for in the spring there is a robin's nest in almost every bank or hedgerow.

You may look for a Tomtit's nest in all sorts of strange places, from a hole in a tree, to a flower-pot which has been thrown away. There will be a number of little white eggs in it speckled with red. The mother will hiss and peck at you to prevent you from taking them away. But in a few days she will not be afraid, for she is a bold little bird.

You must learn to look for other eggs yourselves. In the barn you may find the Owl's large white eggs, and sometimes young birds and eggs together. In a bank of a river, or a hole in a wall, you may find the nest of a Water-wagtail with greyish white spotted eggs. The Rook's bluish green eggs sometimes fall down from their nests; and the Jackdaws will build in your chimneys.

When you have spent some time hunting for nests and eggs, you will notice how cunningly they are hidden by their colour and their marks.

Wherever you find white eggs like those of the owl, the martin, the woodpecker, the kingfisher, and the pigeon, they are either quite hidden in a bank, a tree trunk, or a deep nest, or they are high up out of reach. Most other eggs are spotted, and they are either some shade of green or grey or brown, like the moss and leaves and twigs of the nest.

In any nest you can find, see how many of the eggs grow up into young birds. Choose one nest each, to watch and see which child can count up most young birds.

LESSON V.
BABY BIRDS.

THE mother bird sits on the nest and keeps the eggs warm all the time that the little birds are growing inside. She never leaves them except to stretch herself and get food. Sometimes the father bird sits while she is away, or he brings food to her. Sometimes he only sings to her.

The first thing that the baby-birds do for themselves is to get out of the egg. When they are ready you may hear them crying "cheep, cheep" inside. Then they tap away at the big end with a little horny tip, which grows on the top of their beak, and the shell cracks, and out they come.

If you can catch a chicken as soon as it is out of the egg, you may see this horny tip. But you must be quick, for a chicken is a very active baby-bird. It runs about directly it is hatched, and the horny tip falls off.

The next thing young birds do is to open their beaks and cry for food. Some, like the chickens, ducks, and partridges come out with downy feathers all over them. These run about and get food for themselves. Their mother takes care of them, and they cuddle under her wing when she calls to them.

Others, like the pigeon, the sparrow, and the thrush, are naked, blind, and helpless when they are hatched. They cannot get out of the nest, and their parents have to feed them.

If you keep doves in a cage, or if you can climb up to the pigeon-boxes where the pigeons have their nests, you may learn a good deal by watching a baby pigeon.

The day it comes out of the egg its eyelids are tightly closed. It has only a few downy tufts on its naked body, so you can see

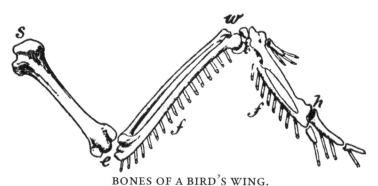

BONES OF A BIRD'S WING.

s. Shoulder.   *e.* Elbow.   *w.* Wrist.   *h.* Hand.   *f.* Feather Quills.

its fleshy wing and feel the bones. Handle it carefully and notice that its wing has three joints, just like your arm. One at the *shoulder (s)* close to the body, one at the *elbow (e)*, and one at the *wrist (w)*.

As it lies in the nest, it draws its elbow back and touches its shoulder with its hand. Then the wing is shut. But if you take hold of the hand (h) gently, and pull the arm out straight, then the wing is open. This is just what a bird does when he stretches his wings to fly.

Now watch the little ones day by day. By degrees pimples come out all over the body. Then the middle of each pimple sinks in and some feathers peep out. The first feathers are quite limp. The little featherlets grow all round the stem like hairs on a cat's tail. These are the down feathers. There are not many on a young pigeon.

BABY BIRDS. – *1.* PARTRIDGE. *2.* KESTREL. *3.* PIGEON.

The next feathers are quite different. They are flat and much stiffer. The featherlets only grow on each side of the stem. They are tinted, and you can see now whether the pigeon is going to be white or coloured.

It is these "covering" feathers which are so beautiful in most birds. They do not grow all over the body. If you push back the feathers of a dead bird you will see that they grow in places only, and spread themselves over the rest.

Meanwhile the long tail and wing feathers have been growing. Those for the tip of the wing grow on the hand, those for the edge of the wing on the arm, between the wrist and the elbow, and above these, like tiles on a roof, grow the small feathers right up to the shoulder, making the wing round and firm.

Feel one of the long wing feathers. It has a strong quill down the middle, which tapers away at the end so that the feather will bend, Now try to pull the featherlets apart. You will find that they stick together, as if they were glued. This is because there are tiny hooks all along each little branch, by which it is hooked on to the next one. So when the wings beat the air, it cannot pass through them, especially as the small side of each feather lies over the broad side of the next one.

A FEATHERED WING.
s. Shoulder.   *e.* Elbow.   *w.* Wrist.

By this time the young pigeons will have opened their eyes. But though they can stand up, they are very weak, and take all their food from their mother.

Then about a month after coming out of the egg, they go to the edge of the pigeon-house and watch the other pigeons. From time to time they stretch out their wings, and flap them a little. As they flap them downwards, the air under the front of the wing cannot get away there, and is driven out behind just as water is driven by an oar when we row. But as they lift the wing up again the feathers turn so that the air can pass through. Therefore, as they flap their wings they raise themselves a little, and flutter to the next ledge, and at last they fly to the ground and begin to pick up food with their parents.

Compare a young pigeon and a young chicken. Examine the down feathers, covering feathers, and long quill feathers.

LESSON VI.

BIRDS FEEDING THEIR YOUNG.

You will find it very interesting to peep into nests and see which birds are naked and which are downy, which can see, and which are blind.

By the river the little Water-hens come out of the egg as black fluffy balls with red heads, and swim away at once after their mother. But Kingfishers come out of the egg naked and helpless. They have to wait till their feathers have grown, before they can leave the nest, and meanwhile their mother feeds them with fish.

Then if you see a young Owl in its nest in a barn, or pick up a young Hawk which has fallen out of a tree, you will find that they are quite blind and helpless, though they are covered with down. Their mothers have to bring them insects, mice, and young rabbits till they are full-grown.

Those of you who live by the seaside know quite well the Gulls which fly out to sea and float on the waves. In the spring and early summer you may hear the young gulls, called Sea-mews or Kittiwakes, mewing like kittens on the ledges of the cliffs. They are calling to their parents to feed them.

For though these young gulls can see and are covered with down, they are born so high up on the cliffs that they must sit and wait till they are strong. Even then they can only creep along the ledges till their wings are full-grown. They sit there with open beaks, crying to be fed, and the old sea-birds bring fish for them to eat. The common gulls, and the herring gulls, generally lay their eggs on islands, and the little ones swim about when they are only a few days old.

Or, if you live far away from the sea in the depths of the country, you will enjoy seeing the other kinds of birds feeding their young ones in the trees and in the hedges. Sometimes the mother does all the work, and sometimes the father takes his share.

Mr. Kearton, who knows so much about birds, tells us that he once helped in the feeding. One day he watched a mother Chiff-chaff bringing food to her five little ones in a nest under a thorn-bush. Chiff-chaffs are very small, graceful birds. Their back and wings are a kind of dull olive green colour, and their breast a yellowish white. The mother was bringing in caterpillars and flies, about four or five every five minutes, and she popped them into the little beaks stretched to reach them. As she worked, her mate flew first to one bough, then to another singing "chiff-chaff, chiff-chaff."

Mr. Kearton thought he would help the little mother. He collected some green caterpillars, and put them on the edge of the nest while she was away. Then he knelt down a little way off.

The mother flew to and fro at her work and looked at him as she passed, but he did not move. At last she picked up the

OWL FEEDING HER LITTLE ONES.

insects he had brought and divided them among the little mouths. Then she flew away for more.

That little mother worked all day long, only resting for half an hour in the afternoon. She not only brought food, but also cleaned the nest between each journey, picking out the pellets of dung, and making everything clean and neat. I think she must have been very glad of the little heaps of insects which her friend put near her nest from time to time.

Tomtits are such bold little birds that you may often see them going in and out of a hole in some wall, or a tree stump, with insects in their mouths. The father and mother Tit both help in feeding. They go out and come back together, laden with caterpillars, and after giving them to the young ones they start off again, calling to each other as they go.

We had some young Robins once which were fed by three birds. They were born in the hedge of our garden. We called the third bird the uncle. He worked quite as hard as the other two. By-and-bye the old robins flew away. But the young ones stayed with us all the summer and used to hop about the dinner table and pick up the crumbs.

Blackbirds feed their baby-birds with large worms, which they pull to pieces, giving a bit to each. The jay looks as if she brought nothing, but she pours the food from her crop into the mouth of the little one. The mother pigeon throws the food up from her crop into her mouth, and the little pigeon puts its beak in at the side of its mother's beak and sucks out the food.

Most parent birds go on feeding the little ones for some time after they can fly. You may often see little sparrows or thrushes sitting in a row on a bough while the mother pops the food into their beaks. She begins at one end and goes quite fairly from one to another, each in its turn.

Watch for birds feeding young in the spring. Thrushes, spar-rows, robins, tomtits. 1. In the nest. 2. Sitting on branches. 3. Small birds feeding a young cuckoo. 4. Young pigeon taking food from the mother.

LESSON VII.
WHERE DO BIRDS SLEEP?

WHERE are all the birds at night? In the daytime we see them in the fields, on the trees and hedges, or on the cliffs. They feed in the garden, the orchard, and the wood. But in the evening, when the sun sets, we hear them singing as if they were saying "good-night," and then they disappear. Only the night birds are about after sunset. Owls hoot and fly after dark, nightingales sing all night in warm summer weather, and if there are any corn-crakes about, you will hear their tiresome cry, "craake, craake," long after you want to go to sleep.

But the other birds are nowhere to be seen. Where are they? It is not easy to find them, for they hide themselves, from fear of the owls, the weasels and the stoats, and they wake and flut-ter away very soon if you come near them.

The small birds sleep chiefly in the hedges. You will be sur-prised how difficult it is to see them, even in winter when the leaves are off the trees; for the twigs and branches crossing each other hide them well. No owl or hawk could seize a bird in a hawthorn hedge.

But how do they keep themselves upon the twigs when

they are fast asleep? If you or I tried to sleep standing up we should fall. For our muscles would grow slack, our heads would nod, and our knees would give way under us.

It is different with a bird. He sits on a branch, and grasps it with his claws. Then he squats down and bends his legs. As he does this, a muscle round his knee-joints pulls the muscles of his toes quite tight, so that his claws are kept clasped round the branch. He cannot move till he has raised himself up and straightened his legs, and thus set his claws free. So the more soundly he sleeps the tighter he grasps the bough, and the less likely he is to fall.

Birds sleep out of doors both summer and winter, and they have a curious covering to keep them warm. It is made of air. When a bird goes to roost, he tucks his head under the plumage of his shoulder, and puffs out his feathers, so that the air gets in between them, and settles all among the soft down which grows close to his body. This air soon becomes warm, and, as it cannot get out, it prevents the bird's warm body from being chilled by the cold air outside.

Still, in bad weather birds often like to find warm nooks to sleep in. House-sparrows, tits, wrens, and other small birds sometimes make holes in hay-stacks for their beds. The owls keep themselves warm in barns, church towers, and sometimes in holes in the trunks of trees. The blue-tit loves to sleep under a thatched roof, and Wrens often hunt up old nests in winter, and huddle together in them to keep themselves warm.

Swallows and swifts do not want to be kept warm, for they fly south in cold weather. In summer they perch on the rafters in the barns, and if you go into a barn after dark, you may of-

BLUE TITS AND YOUNG.

ten hear them flitting from one rafter to another if they are disturbed.

Wood-pigeons roost on the fir-trees in the wood, and hawks on the branches of the taller trees. Pheasants, too, roost in the trees of the wood, and it is curious that they always tell you where they go to bed. For they call "crok, crok," as they settle down to sleep.

CORMORANTS FEEDING.

But partridges sleep on the ground in the fields. They lie in a circle with their heads outwards and their tails together. The father generally sleeps a little way off as a sentinel. Then if a fox, or a weasel, tries to catch them in their sleep, any one that is awake and sees the enemy can give the alarm to the rest.

All these birds sleep inland in the woods and fields. But if you can go to the sea-shore some summer evening and lie on the beach under the high cliffs, you may see other birds coming home to roost. Just as the sun is setting many little birds from the fields perch in the bushes at the top of the rocks. Next come any jackdaws, which happen to live near the sea, cackling and chasing each other over the cliffs. They creep into holes to sleep. Then a few big cormorants sail in from the sea, followed by the gulls, and settle on the ledges half-way down the face of the cliff. Some croaking ravens come flying from the land, and twist and tumble about, before they too sit down for the night. The sand-martins disappear into their holes in the sandstone-rocks, and perhaps a falcon will come circling round in the air and swoop down in some quiet nook.

Then after a time the cackling and the croaking cease and as the moon rises all is quiet. But if you look on the silvery water you will see that many of the gulls are still floating on the waves, and they may remain there all the night.

Watch the birds going to roost at night, and notice their special haunts.

LESSON VIII.
FEEDING IN SUMMER.

SPRING and summer are happy times for birds. Then there is plenty of food for them and their little ones. Let us go out some fine summer morning, and watch the different birds as they feed. You will not see them all in one day. But you ought to find each one some time during the summer.

Close to the house you are sure to see a House Sparrow picking up scraps in the yard and eating the caterpillars and red spiders on the gooseberry bushes in the kitchen garden. For the sparrow is not dainty. He will eat most things, from a grain of wheat to a scrap of meat.

In the kitchen garden, too, you may see the Chaffinch breaking the husks of seeds with his sharp little beak. He is not particular whether he takes them from the weeds, or from the beds of radishes or turnips which we have sown. But he does us more good than harm, for he destroys a great deal of groundsel and chickweed.

Out in the fields the little brown Lark, which has been singing in the sky, drops down to hunt for seeds in the furrows turned up by the plough. In the rickyard I can see several little Finches, the greenfinch and the yellowhammer, picking up the grains of corn.

All these birds feed usually on grain, and have short sharp beaks which will split the husks, though they sometimes eat insects and feed their young ones on them. We have to drive them away from our wheat and oats for a few weeks in the year, but they are very useful in keeping down the weeds, for they eat every seed they can find.

The Swallows, Swifts, and Martins have very different beaks. If you watch them as they skim along in the air, you will see they can open their mouths very wide to catch the flies and gnats. But the hard beak itself is very small. They have weak legs and strong wings, for they catch all their food as they fly. Notice how near the ground they keep in dull weather. Then the insects are flying low, and the swallows follow them. But on a bright day the gnats and midges fly higher, so swallows fly higher too.

That big Thrush which is hopping about on the grass is

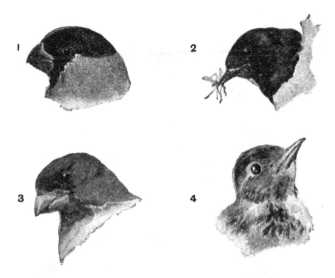

1. BULLFINCH (grain feeder). 2. SWALLOW (fly-feeder).
3. LINNET. 4. LARK (both grain and insect-feeder).

very different from the swallows. He has strong feet and legs, and a long, narrow, round beak. He feeds on worms and snails in the summer, and on berries in the autumn. Look at him now. He has his feet firmly planted on the grass, and he is pulling away at a worm with all his might. He will get it out of the ground soon, and carry it away to feed his little ones.

Many of the smaller perching birds feed only on insects. I am sure you will love them. They are such pretty little things. First, there is the Wagtail with his black and white wings, and his long tail bobbing up and down as he hunts for insects in the grass. Not far off is a little Wren hopping on a rose-tree and picking off the green-fly, which does so much harm.

On a bush near, sits a small brown bird with a grey speckled breast. He only came back to England from warm countries at the end of May. He is the common spotted Fly-catcher. Look how still he sits. Then all at once he darts into the air with wide

SPOTTED FLY-CATCHER.

open mouth, snaps his beak, and goes back to his place. He has caught a fly and will now sit and wait for another.

Next I want you to look at a little bird which I love because he is so bright and gay. He is a Blue Tit or Tomtit, a small bird with a bright blue head and wings, and a yellow breast. He is hanging upside down on the branch of a tree watching for spiders. When he has caught one he will flutter off to another tree and get a good breakfast in a very little while. He is a very bold little bird, and in the winter you may learn to know him well, if you will give him some food.

These birds, the thrush, the wagtail, the flycatcher, the wren and the tomtit are very useful to us. They kill the snails and slugs, the caterpillars, maggots, and grubs. So do the nightingale and the blackbird, and another little bird, which I want you to know. This is the Hedge-sparrow, a small brown bird with a blue-grey breast, which flutters along the lanes. I am sure you must have seen him. He picks up a tiny insect, flits a little way and picks up another, and then flits away again just in front of you as you walk along the lane. You must not confuse him with the house-sparrow. He is quite another kind of bird, he is one of the warblers and sings very sweetly. He is sometimes called the "hedge-warbler," and this is a much better and truer name for him.

We have not much time to watch other birds, But we must look at the rooks hunting for worms and slugs in the ploughed fields; and as we come near the wood I see a partridge feeding on ants under the trees. He flies away with a loud whirr long before we get near him, and as he cries "cluck, cluck" I expect the mother bird and her nest are not far off.

If you go into the wood you may see the little Tree-creeper running up the trees looking for insects, and the woodpecker darting out his sticky tongue and tapping at the trunks of the trees, and the wood-pigeon flying home with her crop full of oats or peas to feed her little ones.

Or if you stroll by the river there may be the tiny kingfisher darting down to seize tiny fish; or the grave heron sitting quite still, with his neck stretched out, till in a moment his head shoots forward, and he brings up a big eel in his beak.

You can notice many of these things for yourselves. The

great secret is to look at every bird you see and try to learn something about it.

Notice the hard beaks of birds which eat seeds—Chaffinch. The hooked beaks of birds which eat flesh—Hawk. The wide gape of birds which catch insects on the wing—Swallow. The long, slender beaks of birds which feel underground for food— Woodcock.

LESSON IX.

MIGRATING IN AUTUMN.

WHEN the summer is over, there is not so much food for the birds, and some begin to go away. Those which live on flying insects go first. The cuckoo is generally gone by the end of July. The swifts start off in August, and about the middle of September the swallows begin to find very few flies, gnats, or moths, and get ready for their long journey.

If you keep a sharp look-out you may see the Swallows and Martins collecting, about the 15th of September, on some church tower, or perhaps on the roof of a barn, and flying off together to roost in the trees. This they never do in the summer. Then they sleep on the rafters of some barn, or under the eaves of a roof, always keeping near buildings. But before they fly away for the winter they gather together in the trees, or on the willows in the osier beds.

Then some morning very early they all disappear. They have started to fly steadily in large flocks, for hundreds of miles, to Africa, where they will have warm weather, and insects to eat, all the winter. You will not see them again till next April.

The little Fly-catchers and the Nightingales go away about

MARTIN AND SWALLOW FEEDING HER YOUNG.

the same time as the swallows, and the Chiff-chaff goes in October. Some of the Wagtails and Robins go too, but not nearly all.

A great many birds shift from place to place in England during the autumn, for food begins to be scarce, and they wander in search of it. Many thrushes and redwings come to us from Norway and Germany, and robins, finches, and other birds come from the north of England to the south. They leave the cold moors and mountains of Cumberland and Yorkshire to feed in Hampshire and Devonshire, where they can find more berries, such as hips and haws, holly-berries, juniper-berries, sloes, and the red berries of the mountain ash. So if you live in the south of England, you may see more robins, thrushes, chaffinches, and yellow-hammers in the winter than you did in the summer.

You will find it very interesting to watch for the different birds, and see when they come and go, and whether you see many or few of any one kind.

You will notice that in winter the little birds move about in flocks, instead of alone, or in pairs, as they do in the summer, when they have their nests and families. In November you will see a great many larks together. The cock-chaffinches sometimes fly in one flock, and the hen-chaffinches in another. The Finches, too, fly in parties; yellow-hammers, greenfinches, and goldfinches all together. They hunt about for seeds, and sleep on the ground, or in the ivy bushes. But the Bullfinches, with their lovely blue-black wings and bright red breasts, keep together in small flocks, flying in a line one after the other along the hedges.

These flocks of different birds flit about from one field to another, keeping together, and scattering over one place at a time, looking for food.

When many of our summer birds have gone to the sunny south, other birds come to us from still colder countries. The Fieldfares fly over from Norway and Sweden. You may see them, in parties of about forty or fifty, wheeling round in the

FLIGHT OF THE SWALLOWS.

air, and settling down on a field to look for grubs and seeds. They are pretty grey birds with brown-red wings and buff speckled breasts. But you cannot often get near enough to see them, for they are very shy. If they hear a noise they are off in a moment, and over the hedge into the next field, where they drop down again to feed. They sleep on the ground; and go back to Norway to build their nests in the spring.

A great many Starlings come from Norway and Germany in the winter, and join those which live with us always. They often fly about with the rooks, but sometimes in flocks by themselves pecking in the fields and chattering one to another.

So when the song-birds are silent in the winter, you can look out for all these other birds and find out where they feed and sleep; when you first see them come, and when you see the last one go. But the thrush and the robin will sing all the year through, when the weather is mild.

Make a list of summer birds which you do not see in the winter. Make a list of winter birds which go away in the spring. Make another list of birds you see all the year round.

LESSON X.
BIRD-FOOD IN WINTER.

WHEN Christmas is past and the real winter cold begins, the poor little birds often have a hard time. So long as the weather is mild, the thrush picks out the slugs and snails from their hiding-places in the walls and palings. The robin and the wren bustle about, looking for seeds and insects. The little wagtails run about the lawns wagging their tails, as they try to find a stray grub, or beetle. In the wood the tree-creeper hunts for spiders and the eggs of insects in the bark of the trees, and the nut-hatches and pigeons feed under the beeches.

But after a while, when a hard frost comes, and snow lies deep on the ground, the birds look very sad. The larks and the linnets crouch down under the banks of the cornfields to keep warm. The thrushes fly from tree to tree to look for a few mistletoe berries, now that all the others are eaten. The chaffinches and the yellow-hammers fly round the farmer's ricks, to pull out some grains of wheat or oats, or grass seeds.

STARLINGS IN WINTER.

The fieldfares wander sadly about in flocks. The rooks, starlings, and jackdaws fly from field to field screaming and cawing as they try to find some place where the wind has blown the snow away and they can peck in the furrows. The lapwings, which you may know by the feathers which stand up on the back of their head, cry "peewit, peewit" mournfully, as they journey to the sea-coast, where they find food on the sands and mudflats at low tide.

It is sad to think how often little birds are starved to death. They do not so much mind the cold, for you remember that the air under their feathers keeps them warm. But in a hard winter they often die from want of food. If you pick up a dead robin, starling, or rook after a long frost, you will find that the bones are only covered with skin and feathers. Its flesh has all wasted away.

Now is your time to be kind to the birds which have sung to you all the summer. They did good work then, eating the caterpillars and grubs, the wire-worms and maggots, the slugs and snails, and keeping down the weeds by eating the seeds. Now you can feed them, for a little while, till the frost and snow are gone.

You will learn to know a great many birds in this way, and you need only give them a few scraps, which you can well spare. Some birds, you will remember, like seeds and crumbs and green food. Others, which eat insects in the summer, will be glad of a little gristle or fat.

So you must save up every scrap from breakfast, dinner, and supper, and keep it for the next morning—crusts of bread, the crumbs off the table, cold potatoes, and potato skins. You can get your mother to boil the potatoes in their skins, and then the birds will like the peel. Perhaps, too, you may save some pieces of cabbage, some apple parings, and a little fat.

All this will make a nice dish for starving birds, if you chop it up and pour a little hot water over the crusts. And if you live on a farm you may be able to sweep up a few grains of corn in the stables, before they are thrown away with the manure.

Then clear the snow away in front of your door, throw the food down and go back out of sight. The birds will soon come, and in a few days they will even be waiting about for their morning meal before you bring it.

BIRDS FEEDING IN WINTER.

You must not forget to hang a piece of fat from the branch of a tree, so that you may see the tits hang head downwards on the string to peck at it. And if you hang up a bone with a little meat on it the starlings and jackdaws will come too.

Then remember that birds want to drink. You can put water for them in a pan, if you change it when it freezes. But if you can spare a few pence to buy a cocoa-nut, you may make it serve two purposes.

Saw it across the middle, and scoop out all the white from one half. Bore two holes near the rim of this cup, and make a handle with a piece of string. Then hang it on a tree and put some water in it. The birds will sit on the rim and drink. And as they make it swing to and fro the water will not freeze. Then hang up the other half in the same way, but leave the white inside. The little tomtits will peck away, and fight for the sweet food till it is all gone.

A number of birds will come—robins, chaffinches, sparrows, wrens, starlings, rooks, jackdaws, thrushes, and many others. You will be able to notice the difference between the big missel-thrush, with his white spotted breast, and the smaller brown song-thrush. And if you put some nuts on the window-sill the nuthatch may come to fetch them if he lives near.

So you will see the birds more closely than you can at any other time, and next summer, when they sing in the trees, they will be old friends.

Make a list of the birds which come to feed at your door in winter.

LESSON XI.
OTHER SMALL BIRDS.

THERE are many other small birds which you may find out for yourselves, but I should like to tell you of a few which are interesting. First there is the little Goldfinch, which is so useful to us because it eats thistle seeds and dandelion seeds. It builds a lovely little nest of fine roots, wool, and horsehair, and often lines it with the soft down of the coltsfoot, that big yellow flower which blooms in the spring and has feathery seed-boxes. The goldfinch has a beautiful red forehead and throat, and black wings barred with yellow, and tipped with white. You may know it from the bullfinch because its breast is pale brown, while the bullfinch has a rich red breast and grey and black wings.

Then there is the cock-Linnet with his crimson breast, brown wings, and a red patch on his head. Linnets change colour at different times of the year. In the winter, the breasts of both birds are grey striped with brown.

All birds moult, that is change their feathers, at least once a year. The father-birds are nearly always more gaudy when they are building their nests. You will notice too that hen-birds are scarcely ever so gay as their mates. This is most likely because they sit on the nests, and it would not do for them to be seen too easily.

Linnets feed in big flocks in the winter. You may see them in the evening dropping down among the gorse and other bushes to sleep. It is sad that both the goldfinch and the linnet are caught and sold to sing in cages. This is why we have not nearly so many in England as we used to have.

I hope you will look out for the Nuthatch, a little bird with a short black beak, a blue-grey back and wings, and a pale yellow breast, shaded with red. He is often seen in orchards and gardens in the autumn, when the nuts are ripe. You may catch sight of him coming down a nut tree, head downwards. He sticks the nuts into the cracks of the trunk and hammers them with his beak to break them. You may sometimes find a little store of nuts which he has hidden at the foot of the tree. He feeds on other things, besides nuts and beech-mast, and he will peck at a piece of bacon in winter, if you hang it out for him.

You must listen for the Blackcap. You will hear him more easily than you will see him. He is a little dark grey bird, with a black head and a pale grey breast, and sings almost as well as a nightingale. He comes back to England in April, and if you listen well you may hear him practising his song. He hides himself in a thick bush and begins gently in a low voice, singing over and over again till he gains strength. In a few days his voice is ready, and he trills out a wild, sweet song all the summer day, flitting from bush to bush as he sings. He feeds on insects and   berries, and brings up four or five lit-tle ones in a lovely nest made of dry grass and spiders' webs, and lined with horsehair. Then he flies away in October till the next spring. But he has been so often caught that he is not so common as he used to be.

Then   there   is   the   little Whitethroat, which creeps along al-most everywhere under the hedges,

BLACK-CAPS IN A
MAPLE BUSH.

and is often called the "nettle-creeper." He too is a brown-grey bird with a little red at the tips of his feathers and on his breast. He hops and flies a little way as the hedge-sparrow does, chattering all the time, and sometimes flying higher and higher and singing louder. He, too, comes in May and goes in October.

There are two other little birds you may very likely see. One is the Stonechat, which lives on commons and sits on the top of the furze bushes. It is a small brown-black bird with white markings and a rusty red breast. It cries "chat, chat, chat," and hides its nest so well in the gorse bushes that you will scarcely find one.

The other is the little Dipper or water-ouzel, which hops about the stones in the bed of rapid streams and rivers. It feeds on insects and water snails. It is a black bird not quite as big as a thrush, with a very short tail and a snowy-white breast. It has a curious way of dipping its head down and flirting its tail.

There is not room to tell about magpies or jays, but if you have any near you, you will know them already.

Find out these small birds and any others in your neighbourhood, and try to know their nests and eggs.

LESSON XII.

BIRDS OF PREY.

WE call "Birds of Prey" those which feed on the smaller animals, such as rabbits, mice, frogs, and snakes, as well as on other birds. The chief kinds in our country are eagles, falcons, hawks, and owls.

If you live in the mountains of Scotland, or the north of England, you may, perhaps, have seen an eagle. But the birds of prey you are most likely to know are hawks and owls.

I am sure that sometimes when you are in the fields, you must have seen a bird with long pointed wings and a tail like a fan hovering in the air. This is the Kestrel or common hawk. Country people call him the "wind-hover." His wings beat the air so quickly that you can scarcely see them move, yet he keeps quite still in the same place. His bright eyes look eagerly on the ground. Now he darts a little up or down, and floats along some distance. Now he hovers again, and all at once drops to the ground. He has seen a mouse in the grass, and rises up with it in his claws.

Farmers often shoot kestrels because they steal young partridges and chickens, when they cannot find other food. But they are very useful in killing field-mice, moles, beetles, and all kinds of vermin.

If you cannot tame a young hawk, nor find a dead one, you can see how to know a bird of prey. Look at the long toes and sharp claws of the eagle or the hawk. They pierce the skin of any animal he seizes. His hooked beak is very strong, and has sharp edges, so that it cuts like shears. The upper half is pointed, and hangs over the lower half. A few strong pecks with this cruel beak soon kill the tiny mouse or larger animals, which are swallowed whole or torn to pieces. After a little time the furry skins and the bones are thrown up in a ball. The feet and legs of a bird of prey are covered with scales, so that when he is fighting he is not so much hurt by hard pecks.

The kestrel's wings are strong and pointed, and he can fly quickly, or keep himself floating, as he pleases. He is about as large as a wood-pigeon. His back and wings are a bright brick-red, and his tail is grey, tipped with white, with a black band across. The long feathers of his wings are black, while his breast is pale yellow.

GOLDEN EAGLE.

Another common hawk is the Sparrow-hawk, which has dark grey wings and a reddish-brown breast with orange stripes. He does not often hover, but glides along the hedges looking for birds and mice. He does more harm than the kestrel, for he often kills game. But he is useful in destroying mice, and insects, and in preventing the small birds, which eat the corn, from becoming too numerous. The mother sparrow-hawk is much larger than the father.

Owls, like hawks, have hooked beaks and long sharp claws. But their beak is not so strong, and their feet are more useful for climbing. Their four toes stand, three in front and one behind, like most birds, but they can turn back the outer front toe so as to have two in front and two behind, like the wood-pecker.

Notice too the difference in their eyes. A hawk has his eyes on the sides of his head, but the owl has his in front of his face like you or I. So, when he hunts in the twilight, he can peer down at things close to him. He can make the pupil of his eye as large as the cat does, so as to gather all the light there is. His feathers are so soft and downy that he makes very little noise as he flies, and he has large hidden ears with flaps over them, and can hear the slightest sound. Some owls have ear tufts sticking up in the air like a cat's ear.

The owl you hear so often crying "to-whoo, to-whoo" is the brown or Tawny Owl. He hunts in the early morning and late evening. In the day-time he hides in holes of the trees and in church towers. If he is driven into the sunlight he winks and blinks, and cannot see clearly. But in the dusk, or the moon-light he flies noiselessly along the hedges, and catches mice,

BARN OWL AND KESTREL HAWK.

moles, frogs, and birds, swallowing the small ones whole and throwing back the feathers and skin in little balls.

The Barn Owl is a much lighter bird than the brown owl. His back and wings are buff colour and his breast and face are white. He cries "te-whit, te-whee" in a loud screech, and is therefore often called the "Screech Owl." He hides in the barn, or in trees, by day and hunts by night, feeding chiefly on mice. When he comes out by daylight the chaffinches and other little birds tease him, for they know he cannot see well.

Compare a hawk and an owl. Notice the cere, or piece of bare skin at the top of the beak, which all birds of prey have. It is partly covered by bristles in the owls. Try to draw the foot and beak of the eagle.

LESSON XIII.
ROOKS AND THEIR COMPANIONS.

"You go and scare they rooks out o' that field. They be eating all the seed," I heard a Devonshire farmer say to his boy one day. He was quite right. He had not sown his wheat deep enough, and the rooks were feeding on it.

But some time after another farmer pointed to the rooks in his field, where the corn was green. "See how they be pulling up they young oats," said he. And so they were. But when we looked at the plants which they had pecked up, we found that each one had a place in the root where a grub had been living.

This time the rooks had been doing useful work. Wireworms and other grubs eat away the roots of grass, corn, and turnips all across a field. When the rooks kill a few grubs, they often save the whole crop.

Once, a long time ago, some Devonshire farmers gave a large reward for rooks' heads, thinking they did harm to the farms. All the rooks around were soon killed. But the farmers were sorry afterwards. During the next three years all their crops were destroyed by insects and grubs. They had to persuade some fresh rooks to build in their neighbourhood to keep down the insects.

No doubt rooks do some mischief, for they eat birds' eggs, and newly sown corn, new potatoes, and green walnuts. They even sometimes pull grain out of the stacks, when they are short of food. But they destroy so many wire-worms and grubs, snails and slugs, maggots and insects of all kinds, that they do more good than harm.

You all know the heavy whirring cockchafer, which flops into your face in the evening. But perhaps you do not know that before he had wings he lived for three or four years underground feeding on the roots of grass and corn. Rooks eat these cockchafer grubs wherever they can find them, and so save our crops.

I hope you have rooks near you, for they are delightful to watch. When they build their huge nests high up in the forks of trees, they make a great deal of noise and bustle. The father-rook begins to fetch food for his mate even before she lays her eggs, and feeds her all the time she is sitting.

The old birds feed the young ones long after they are hatched. If you watch, you may see the young ones sitting on the edge of the nest opening their mouths to be fed. Rooks like to build near old houses, and use the same nests year after year. They will not allow strange rooks to join them.

ROOKS IN A ROOKERY.

If the trees in which they build lose their leaves in winter, the rooks do not stay there long after the last young ones are able to fly. About August or September they often go to the beech and pine woods to sleep, and do not come back to their rookery till the spring. But every now and then on their way to and fro they call at their rookery and look after their nests.

Crows do not live together in numbers like rooks. They live in pairs, and build their nests in the top of some high tree away from houses. They are more mischievous than rooks, for they feed on birds and young lambs, young pigeons, ducks, or chickens.

You may tell a crow from a rook at a distance because you very seldom see more than two together. When you can see them near, you will know them apart, because the rook, after he is a year old, has a bald patch on his head just above his beak, where the crow has feathers.

Have you ever noticed how gravely a rook walks across a field? He does not hop like a thrush or a sparrow, but moves one foot after the other, and gives a little jump every now and then. One or two always remain on the trees near, to give notice of danger, and when these sentinels cry "caw-caw" the whole flock rises. They fly away, flapping

JACKDAWS.

their wings slowly, and drop down one by one in another field.

A friend of mine who lives near a rookery says she often sees from her window one or two sentinel rooks go round every morning and wake up the others, and it is very funny to see how the lazy ones scramble up in a great hurry at the last, so as to be in time to fly away with the rest.

Though rooks will not allow another party of their own kind to join them, they allow starlings, jackdaws, and fieldfares to feed with them. A Jackdaw moves much like a rook, though he is a more sprightly bird. He is smaller and has a grey patch on his head. The Starling is a walking bird. Though his head and back are black, he has so many bright colours on the tips of his feathers that he does not look so dark as the rook and the jackdaw, but very bright and gay.

I wonder why these birds like so much to follow the rooks? Perhaps it is because the rook has a keen scent, and turns up the earth for food with his long beak. The jackdaw and starling only pick up what they find above ground, so when the rook turns up the earth, they may get some of the food.

Try to see a rook, a crow, a jackdaw, and a starling, a magpie and a jay, and point out how you know them apart.

LESSON XIV.
WEB-FOOTED BIRDS.

BESIDES the birds which live and feed on the land there are a great many which live mostly on the water. Some of these are called "waders," and some are "swimmers" and have webbed feet. We read about two waders, the coot and the moorhen, in Book II. To-day we will talk about the swimming birds.

If you live by the seaside, you will know the gulls which float on the sea, and often fly a long way up the rivers. Gulls come up the river Thames as far as London, and feed in the ponds of the parks. In the winter it is a pretty sight to watch them circling round and round, and catching the food which people throw to them.

You may have seen Cormorants, big black birds which fly heavily over the sea, with their long necks stretched out and their narrow wings beating the air. Then they settle on the water, and suddenly jump up and dive down head foremost, presently coming up with a fish, which it takes them often some time to swallow.

But if you live in the country near a large lake or a river, you are more likely to see a curious little swimming bird called the little Grebe or dabchick. This is a brown bird with a thin neck

FEET OF BIRDS.
1. Bird of Prey–*Eagle*.   *2.* Web-footed–*Goose*.
3. Scratching–*Pheasant*.   *4.* Climbing–*Woodpecker*.
5 & 6. Perching–*Missel-thrush* and *Lark*.

and head, which paddles about among the reeds on the bank of a river, or swims along quietly, diving down every now and then to catch water-snails, fish, or weeds. You will have to move very quietly if you want to get near the dabchick, for it dives down at the least alarm and comes up a long way off, out of sight.

If you have not seen any of these web-footed birds, nor even a wild duck yet every child knows the tame Duck which lives in our farmyards. Our ducks and drakes were tamed long, long ago from wild ducks, and are still very like them. Let us see what we can learn about a duck.

First I want you to look at her as she waddles across the yard. Her feet have a skin between the three front toes which joins them together. That is to say she is "web-footed." Now notice that, as she lifts her foot, the skin folds up like a fan, and when she puts her foot down, it spreads out again. When she reaches the pond, she glides into the water and begins to paddle, using one foot after the other, just as you do when you walk. In clear water you can see that as she puts her foot forward the skin shuts up, as it did when she walked, but when she puts it back and strikes the water, it opens and makes a paddle, and so she rows herself along.

Her legs grow far back on her body, so that she can use them to twist and turn herself about, and she can tip her head and body down into the water to look for water-snails and tadpoles, while she paddles along with her tail up in the air.

Next notice how light her body is. It floats quite on the top of the water. This is partly because she has a layer of light fat under her skin, and partly because she has a thick covering of down under her feathers. There is a great deal of air caught in this down, and this makes her light.

Do you know why her feathers do not get wet and draggled in the water? The reason is very curious. Her outer feathers are all smeared with oil which she gets from a little pocket near her tail. Look at her when she comes out of the water. She presses her beak against her tail and then draws the feathers through the beak. When she has oiled them in this way, they are waterproof and keep the wet off her body.

SEA GULLS AND YOUNG.

Next watch her as she feeds. She goes gobble, gobble through the mud, and often throws her head up to swallow something she has found. Her beak is broad and flat. It is hooked at the tip, but higher up it is covered with a soft skin full of nerves. With this skin the duck feels what is in the mud as well as if she saw it. The tip and edges of the beak are very horny and sharp, and, both above and below, it is lined with thin strips of horn. When she closes her beak these strips fit into each other and make a strainer. With her sharp beak she cuts the weeds or kills the snails. With the strainer she sifts the mud and keeps the food in her mouth, forcing out the water with her thick tongue. Geese, swans, and all wild ducks have feet and beaks much like our farmyard duck.

You may have seen wild-ducks in the lakes or rivers. The drake is a very handsome bird. His head and neck are a dark shiny green. He has a white collar, and his breast is the colour of a chestnut. His wings and back are partly brown and partly green. The four middle feathers of his tail are a glossy black and curl up. The others are grey, edged with white. When the wild drake changes his coat in June he puts off this beautiful plumage, and puts on a plain brown and grey suit, like the mother duck, till August. Then he begins to moult again, and in October is as gay as before.

a. DUCK'S HEAD. *b*. A BILL SHOWING THE EDGES OF THE STRAINER.

The cormorants and gulls have not beaks like

the duck, for they do not grope in the mud. Their bills are sharp and strong for fishing, and their wings long for flying. The little dabchick, on the contrary, has short wings, as he chiefly floats on the water. His beak is not very long, and it has no hook at the end. His feet are rather large, but the web is not wide as in ducks.

There are a great many other web-footed birds. Try if you can find some.

Examine a dead duck. Notice the webbed foot, the parts of the beak, the thick down, and the glossy oiled feathers not wetted in water. Draw the foot of any dead bird you can find.

LESSON XV.
BIRD ENEMIES.

ALMOST every morning, when I wake, I hear a curious cry, "tek-tek-tek," in my garden, and I know that if I go out and look, I shall see the cat about somewhere. Sometimes many birds will be making the same cry all together, and when the cat is on the lawn I have seen the swallows swoop down and peck her back, and then rise up again before she can turn round.

For the birds know very well that the cat is their enemy, and scold at her when she comes near, especially when they have young ones.

I wonder if you have ever thought as you lie snugly in bed how many dangers there are for the little birds outside? The owl prowling along the hedge is on the look-out for sitting mothers and for young birds. The cat may climb the tree and put her sharp claws into the nest. Weasels and stoats are hunting about to catch any birds which are sleeping near the ground, or even in the trees, and snakes like eggs for their early breakfast as much as you or I do.

The fox is a great enemy of the ground birds. Partridges, pheasants, and grouse dread a fox at night, as the fowls and

STOAT HUNTING YOUNG ROBINS.

ducks do in the farmyard; while in the daytime the hawk is a terror to all birds. The mother lark, on her nest, crouches down in the hope that the grass may hide her. The father lark, as he soars, rises or falls to try to escape. Other little song-birds flutter away to the bushes; partridges run to cover, and pigeons hide in the wood when a hawk is near.

All these are the birds' natural enemies; for of course animals must kill their food, and we too kill birds to eat. But we need not destroy their nests nor take their eggs for show, nor catch them, as many do, in nets to put them in cages, or to use their feathers for ornaments.

Many birds, which were quite common thirty years ago, are rare now because such a number of eggs and birds have been taken. So laws have been made to protect the little song-birds, birds of prey, and sea-birds, as well as partridges and pheasants.

All over England people are now forbidden to shoot or snare any wild birds except on their own land, or to take their eggs, between the 15th of March and 1st of August. This leaves the birds time to bring up their little ones. And there is a special list of birds which people may not disturb, even in their own garden, during this "close time."

I am sure you will be glad to know that the lark is one of these birds.

Then there are some parts of England where people are not allowed to take the eggs of wild birds at any time. These are places, such as some of the Broads in Norfolk, and the seashore at Slapton Lee in Devonshire, where many birds breed.

You cannot know all these places, but there is one very safe rule. Do not take any eggs, nor kill any birds; then you are sure not to do wrong.

Watch the birds in the garden, and the fields, and the woods. Learn to know where they build their nests round your house, and take care they are not disturbed. When you wake up in the morning listen to their songs. You will soon know them, and know too when they are happy, or when something is frightening them. Then notice what good work they do, eating the slugs and snails, the wire-worms and grubs.

You must drive them away when you see them eating your seeds, or your young buds, or the sprouting corn. But you can feed them in winter to make them your friends, and you will be surprised how much you can learn about their ways.

BOOK V
TREES AND SHRUBS

"EYES AND NO EYES"

Fifth Book.

TREES AND SHRUBS.

LESSON I.
THE VALUE OF TREES.

I WONDER if you have ever stopped to think how useful trees are in the world. We saw in Book III. that plants make the air pure for us to breathe. Trees, with their hundreds of leaves, do a large part of this work, and they do a great deal besides.

Let us imagine a little tree growing up in the wood, or in the field. It may perhaps be eaten away by rabbits or squirrels before it is a year old. If so, it has been useful as food. But if it grows up, it begins even the first year to drop some leaves in the autumn, and these help to make leaf-mould, and so give food for other plants.

So it goes on each year, making leaves, purifying the air, and producing leaf-mould. But very soon insects begin to make their home in the young sapling, for every kind of tree has some insects living on it. A moth comes and lays her eggs under the leaves, and the caterpillars feed on them when they are hatched. A beetle comes and lays her eggs in the bark, and the grub feeds there, till it turns into a beetle, or till the woodpecker or the nuthatch find and eat it.

In this way every tree is quite a little colony of living creatures. Then the birds come and sleep in its boughs at night and
build their nests there in the spring. If the trees are elms the
rooks often choose them for their rookery. If they are firs in a
wood the wood pigeon will sleep there, or pheasants and
hawks perch on their branches, while the thrush and the blackbird spend the night in laurels, or hollies and other evergreen
trees.

When the tree has grown big it bears flowers and fruits.
These fruits, or the seeds in them, serve as food for many creatures. The birds feed on the berries, the nuts, and the acorns.
The squirrel makes its home in the beech-trees, and eats all
kinds of nuts it can find. The field-mouse, hedgehog, and pig
make good meals off the beech-nuts and acorns on the ground,
while we eat the fruit of the sweet chestnut and the walnut
tree, the apples, pears and cherries from the orchard.

How useful the trees are to man! They help to keep the
ground moist and fresh. There is always more rain in a country
where there are trees, and the ground would grow parched and
dry, if it were not for their pleasant shade. How the cattle
gather under them, when the sun is bright, and stand chewing
the cud so peacefully out of the glare and heat! And how glad
you are on your way to school, if you can walk through a shady
lane instead of along the high road. Then they are so beautiful
in the spring; when the fresh green leaves burst out they make
us glad to think that every year tree-life begins again.

On the other hand, some trees are so old, several hundreds
of years, that they remind us of times long gone by, and make

us love our country when we think what a long history those trees could tell.

But even trees must die at last, and, if they are to be of use to us we must cut them down before they decay. Then, after the tree is dead, how useful it is!

Let us just go through one day of your life, and see how much of a tree you use. You get up in the morning, and the first thing to be done is to light a fire with wood. You sit on a chair: that is made of wood. You open the door that is of wood too. You take up your umbrella when you start for school: the handle was once the bough of a tree. You go upstairs to fetch your bag: the stairs are made out of planks. You set off on your way, and have to cross a brook: the bridge is made of wood. You are careful to shut the gate of the field: that, too, is made of a tree, and so is the paling round the school.

You take your place in class. Your feet rest on deal planks which come from the fir-tree. You sit on a wooden bench. Your slate has a wooden frame. Your pen has a wooden handle. The teacher puts up a wooden easel and a wooden blackboard upon it. She opens the ink-bottle to fill the inkstands, and the cork of the bottle comes from the bark of a tree, while the ink itself is made with acid which comes from a gall made by an insect on an oak-tree.

Dinner-time comes. Surely, now, you will not want any wood. You fetch your basket with your dinner in it. That may be made of wood-chips or willow twigs, and the pastry which you eat is made of paste, which your mother rolled out on a wooden board with a wooden rolling-pin.

As you come out from school you get a lift in a farm-cart,

that too is made of wood, and so is the wheelbarrow you use, when you get home, for wheeling manure into the garden. You put your school things away in the old oak-chest in the corner, and when you go to bed after supper, you look up at the old beams across the ceiling and fall asleep dreaming of wood everywhere.

You could add many more things that I have forgotten; and even now we have not reckoned up the gums, the turpentine, the oils, the tannin, and the many sweet scents which we get from trees. Nor have we spoken of boats, and railway carriages, nor of the beautiful wood-carvings in our churches and other public buildings. Surely the world would get on very badly without trees!

Name any things made of wood besides those given in the lesson.

LESSON II.
HOW A TREE STARTS.

We saw in Book III. that some plants live much longer than others. Some live for one year only, make their seeds and die. These we call annuals. Others live two years. They grow their roots and leaves one year, and flower and make their seeds the next year. These we call biennials, because bi means two. Others live for many years, and are called perennials. Trees are perennials, for they live for very many years. There are some oak trees more than a thousand years old.

Yet all these old trees began their lives as little seedlings, like the bean you grew on the top of the earth in the flower-pot.

How, then, have they managed to live so long? We shall learn this best by looking at a young seedling.

If you poke about in a wood, you will easily find some small plant, either of oak, or beech, or hazel, which has grown up from a nut, or an acorn trodden into the ground. I am going to take an oak tree, because I have one close to my door and can give you a picture of it. If you get an acorn and stick it in the neck of a bottle, the same way up as it sits in its cup, and keep the bottle full of water, you can grow a small oak for yourself, and see if yours is like mine.

First the acorn puts out some roots downwards. Then the husk splits, and you can see the two thick seed-leaves open, with the growing tip between them. This tip now grows steadily upwards and soon puts forth leaves. There may be one, or even two, one above the other, on the sides of the stem. But there will certainly be two or three close together at the top of the little tree by the time autumn comes.

YOUNG OAK PLANT.
1. Growth of 1st year.
2. Growth of 2nd year.
3. Growth of 3rd year.
r. Ring left by scales of buds.

At the foot of each leaf, nestling up to the stem, will be a little nestling up to the stem, will be a little bud, and at the end of the stem will be a stout bud, bigger than all the rest.

The difference between the oak-plant and the bean which we grew in Book III. is that the stem is woody. If you get another oak-plant of the same age from the wood, and cut off its head this is what you will see (Fig. 1, page 6). In the middle there is a round white patch, *p*. This is the *pith*, or soft part, which you scoop out of the branch of an elder-tree when you make a popgun. Next comes a ring of soft whitish *wood*, *w*. Outside this again is the *bark*, *b*.

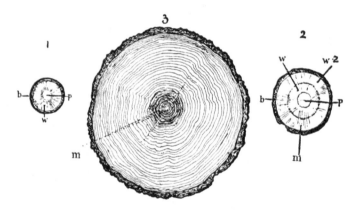

OAK STEMS CUT ACROSS.

1. Twig of 1st year.   *2.* Twig of 2nd year.   *3.* Trunk of an old Oak with rings of growth.   *p.* Pith.   *w.* Wood   *b.* Bark
w 2. Wood of 2nd year.   *m.* Medullary or Pith ray.

Now you know that water, with earthy matter in it, has to rise up from the roots and go to the leaves, to be made into food. It travels up through this ring of living wood, and when it comes back it makes new wood and new bark just where the wood and the bark meet. You know how easy it is to peel the bark off wood. That is because the tender new part is between them, and gives way easily.

But as soon as autumn comes, the roots leave off taking in water; and the crude *sap*, as it is called, does not rise up any more. The stalks of the leaves dry up where they join the stem, and they fall off. The tree rests for the winter.

Now watch your little plant next sprung. You will see the big bud at the tip, and often two other buds close to it, begin to grow into branches and have leaves of their own. But in a very young tree the smaller ones usually die away and the trunk grows straight up. However, you can always tell where the new growth began in the spring, because there is a ring (r, page 5) left by the scales of the buds. The wood of the new piece will be just like the wood of the lower piece was last year. But that lower piece will be growing some fresh wood and getting bigger (Fig. 2, page 6). The sap will go up and down as before, and a new ring of wood (*w 2*) will form *outside* the old wood, and a very thin new ring of bark *inside* the old bark. So at the end of the second year, while the new piece will have only one ring of wood, the old piece below the scales will have two rings (*w* and *w2*), with a mark between the rings, showing where the tree rested in the winter.

All this is rather difficult to see in such small trees, and you must look at the diagrams. But if you go into the wood when they are cutting down timber, you will see the rings much more distinctly in the older trees, and you will like to look at the trunks, and try to make out how old the trees are. You cannot be quite sure that you count all the years, because as the new wood grows, the old is squeezed together, and makes a very hard wood, called "heart-wood," in the middle of the trunk. But you can be sure that the tree is not younger, and most likely much older, than the rings you can count.

Now to come back to our question, how trees live to be so old. Year after year they make a new ring of wood, narrower and narrower its they grow older. Through the younger rings the crude sap goes up to the leaves, and the food-sap comes down to feed the parts of the tree. Buds are formed every spring on the stems at the foot of each leaf, and these buds are like new plants. They start with fresh strength, making new food for the tree, which carries them up on its trunk and branches into the light and air.

The heart-wood of the tree is really dead, and sometimes decays away while the outer part of the tree is still flourishing. But many of the rings of wood far inside the trunk still want food, and if you look at a felled tree you can see how they get it. Besides the rings, you will see some lines (*m*), like the spokes of a wheel, starting from the centre of the trunk and spreading out to the bark. These lines are made of pith, like that we saw in the middle of the young seedling oak. Until they are squeezed away the sap passes along them all through the tree.

There are some trees, such as the palms, which you see in hot-houses, which do not grow in rings. But these are not English, and do not concern us here.

Get several pieces of tree-branches and try to see the bark, the inner bark, the rings of wood and the heart-wood—Lilac, Lime, and Elder show the parts well. Oak and Pine show heart-wood best.

LESSON III.

HOW A TREE GROWS. — THE HORSE-CHESTNUT.

WHEN a young tree has made plenty of wood and branches, it begins to use some of its buds for making flowers. These buds grow in the same places as leaf-buds. In some trees they grow where the leaf joins the stem. In others they grow at the tips of the twigs. They are generally rounder and less pointed than the leaf-buds.

The flowers of the oak are very small, so you had better look out for a horse-chestnut tree and gather a bough for this lesson. You will find buds on a horse-chestnut tree almost any time in the year, except when it is in full leaf, and then they will be very small.

The best time to look is just at the end of the winter, when the tree is bare. First notice the smaller buds, which grow two and two opposite each other along the twig. You will see below each bud a scar marking the place on which the leaf grew last year. This scar is shaped like a horseshoe, and has several black spots on it arranged like the nails. These spots show where the bundles of tubes were, which carried the sap into the leaf.

Now pick one of the buds to pieces. They are small, and you will not find it very easy, but you can take off the brown sticky scales, and you will find inside, first some soft gummy down, and then the young green leaves, tightly folded together, with a green growing tip between them.

So if you had left that bud, and it could get food enough, it would have grown into a small branch in the spring, with leaves on it. But it is very seldom that all the buds on a branch

grow. The stronger ones take the food, and the weaker ones either die or wait till next year.

Now look at the buds on the tips of the branches. They are
very much larger than those growing on the sides, and you can
examine them easily. When you have taken away from twelve
to seventeen sticky scales, you will come to the same kind of

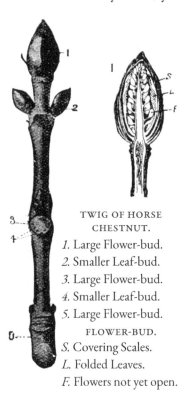

soft white gummy down which
you found in the leaf-buds,
making a warm bed for the tender growing parts inside.

But this bud is not all leaves
like the smaller one. It has four
small bright green leaves, and
wrapped up inside them is a
tiny spike covered with little
knobs *(F)*.

You cannot examine the
flowers on this spike without a
microscope. But if you wait
and watch till May, you will see
others like it gradually opening
out into a lovely branch of
flowers, and I think you will

TWIG OF HORSE
CHESTNUT.

1. Large Flower-bud.
2. Smaller Leaf-bud.
3. Large Flower-bud.
4. Smaller Leaf-bud.
5. Large Flower-bud.
FLOWER-BUD.
S. Covering Scales.
L. Folded Leaves.
F. Flowers not yet open.

like them all the better for knowing how the tree prepared
them last autumn, when it was covered with leaves, and
wrapped them up warm all the winter in sticky buds.

And while you are waiting for the flowers, look at the tree
itself. The trunk is smooth and round. The branches begin to
grow out of it about ten feet from the ground. They grow two

HORSE-CHESTNUT FLOWER AND FRUIT.

and two opposite to each other like the leaves, except where a bud has failed. The lower branches, which of course are the oldest, stretch out farthest, so that the tree rounds off very gracefully up to the top.

Then, as April comes, the brown scales fall from the leaf-buds, and the tree is covered with bright green downy leaves. They are each cut into seven leaflets, which hang down from the tip of the leaf-stalk like a half-opened umbrella. Little by little, as they grow stronger, they rise up into a broad leaf with seven fingers. It is while they are doing this that the flower-buds throw off their scales, the four green leaves open out, and the flower spike begins to hang out its snow-white flowers, streaked with pink and yellow.

The flowers nearest to the branch open first and grow strong. They are perfect flowers, with five green sepals and five beautiful crimped petals, and have both stamens and seed-box inside. These will form the chestnuts which ripen in the autumn. The flowers nearer to the tip of the spike have only stamens inside the petals. They wither away as soon as they have shed their pollen-dust.

If you can get an old flower spike when the flowers are withered, and cut the seed-box of a flower across, you will see that it has three divisions with two little seeds in each. But when you pick up the prickly fruit in the autumn, though it burst into three parts, there are generally only two horse-chestnuts inside, with another very tiny one. The two big seeds have starved out the other four little ones and grown big and strong. If the chestnuts are brown and shiny, they are ripe, and will grow if you sow them.

Though the horse-chestnut is very beautiful in the summer, its leaves turn yellow very early and fall in August, and then you can see the buds already formed for next year. All boys know that horse-chestnuts are bitter and not good eating. The sweet chestnuts, which we roast, come from quite a different tree, and are not seeds, but fruits.

Bring a branch of horse-chestnut and examine the buds. Find a flower spike in May; look at the ovary in June, and the fruit in September.

LESSON IV.
TREES WITH CATKIN FLOWERS.

THE horse-chestnut is the only big English tree which has large flower-spikes. There are many pretty flowering shrubs in the hedge, such as the Blackthorn, the May, and the Guelder rose. But all the big trees have tiny flowers. As some of these trees flower before they open their leaves, you can see their blossoms. So we will look at a few.

If you live where there are many bees, and where there are any trees of the common Sallow Willow growing in the hedges, or the woods, go out some sunny day in March, and lie down under one of the trees and listen.

Before long you will bear a buzzing, which will go on as long as the sun is bright. For the bees have wakened from their long winter sleep, and want honey and pollen to make bee-bread. There are very few flowers open in March and, as the sweet smell of honey comes from the blossoms of the willow, the bees are quick to find them out.

Perhaps you will ask me how you are to know a Sallow Willow. You know it quite well, though you may not know the name. It is a big shrubby tree, with a purple-brown stem, which grows in the hedges and woods, and from which people cut branches before Palm Sunday, and call them palms. All up the twigs you will see in March and April round soft bodies about as big as thimbles growing now on one side now on the other. It is into these that the bees are poking their heads. You remember the catkins which we saw on the nut-trees in Book I. These soft bodies clinging close to the willow stems are also catkins. In willows they stand up, instead of hanging down as they do on the nut-trees, and on the sallow willow they hug the stem.

But now I want you to look a little further. The tree under which you sit may have broad yellow catkins, and if you gather a branch and look closely at it, you will see the yellow anthers standing out all round the catkin. Children call these "golden palms." But you may find, not so very far away, another of the same kind of tree, on which the catkins are soft and grey. They are much longer and narrower than the golden catkins. Children call them "silver pussy-palms."

Gather a branch from each of these trees and take them to school. When you pick them to pieces, you will find that each catkin is made up of a number of tiny flowers. In the golden catkins each flower is only a little scaly leaf (*L, 2*) with two stamens growing on it. No! I forgot. There is something else, for at the bottom of each scaly leaf is a small cup (*H*), holding a drop of honey. So you see there are plenty of drops of honey in a catkin.

Then if you pick the silver-pussy-palm to pieces, you will

find the same honey cup (*H*) at the bottom of the scale, but instead of stamens, there is a little seed-box or ovary (*O*) shaped like a bottle, with a crumpled stigma (*S*).

Now you see the use of the honey. As the dust-bags and the seed-boxes are on different trees, the flowers have to tempt the bees to carry the pollen. It is wise to plant willows near where bees are kept, for they get plenty of honey from them in the spring. The Osier willow, which grows in the marshes, and is used for making baskets, is in bloom at the same time as the sallow. But the common English willow which grows into a large tree, and the Crack willow whose branches break off so easily when you bend them, bloom later, when their narrow pointed leaves are out. They all bloom

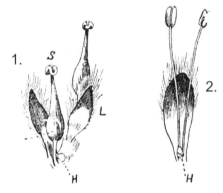

FLOWERS OF THE SALLOW WILLOW.
1. Flower with Ovary. *2.* Flower with Stamens. *L.* Leaf-scale. *H.* Honey-cup. *O.* Ovary. *S. Stigma*

early, however, and when the tiny seeds covered with down are blown out of the catkins many a little bird uses them to line its nest.

Another tree, which blooms before its leaves come, is the English poplar, which grows by the streams, or in the woods. Poplars have their two kinds of flowers on different trees, like the willows. But they have no honey, and no bees come near them. I think that if you have any poplars in your woods and watch them, you will guess how they manage. For when the

SALLOW WILLOW.

1. Silver Pussy Palm bearing the Ovaries.   *2.* Golden Palm bearing Anthers.

wild March winds are blowing, the long hanging catkins swing to and fro, and the dry pollen-dust is blown through the air from tree to tree.

I wonder if you know which tree I mean by the English poplar? Not those tall stiff trees which point straight up to the sky. Those come from Italy and are called Lombardy poplars. The English poplars are graceful trees with very broad leaves

TWIGS OF ENGLISH POPLAR.
1. Catkins with Anther Flowers. *1a*. One Flower enlarged.
2. Catkins with Ovary-bearing flowers. *2a*. One Flower enlarged.

hanging on long stalks. The white poplar has soft white hairs under its leaves, and the leaves of the aspen or trembling poplar are silky underneath. The leaves turn on their long stalks when the wind blows and look very pretty as they show their white sides.

One other tree you must look for, which has its stamens in long loose catkins and its ovary in a little bud with scales round it. This is our friend the oak after it has grown into a large tree. The oak flowers in the spring, just as the leaves are coming out. You will easily see the catkins waving in the wind, but the flowers which will grow into acorns are very small and grow singly, or in pairs, between the leaf-stalk and the stem. Each one has a number of small scales round it, which by-and-by will harden into the cup of the acorn.

But the oak is such an important tree that we must talk of it in a separate lesson.

Bring willow branches in March with stamen-catkins, and others with seed-forming catkins. Look for the honey cup. Bring leaves and flowers of the English poplar.

LESSON V.
THE BRITISH OAK.

I WONDER if you have any woods near you with oak trees growing close together, or mixed with beech and ash trees. This is the way they are grown, when they are to be cut into long planks, or poles, and most likely there will be some wood, where you can stop and look at them on your way home from school.

They will have straight, smooth trunks; some twenty, some thirty, some perhaps fifty feet high, before the branches spread out above. Yet you know that your seedling oak has buds, first on one side, then on the other, all up the stem. How is it that these buds have not grown into branches?

The reason is that in a thick wood, where the trees crowd

each other, every tree wants to raise its head up to the light. So in the spring when the leaves and buds open out at the top of the little tree, and the crude sap rises up to them from the roots, the tree wants so much to use for growing up higher that only a small quantity goes down again to make new wood. So the buds lower down do not get enough food to grow, and they either die or become dormant. That is, they remain waiting for another opportunity, which often never comes. For this reason oaks in a wood grow taller and taller with only a crown of branches and leaves near the top.

But if you can find an old oak out in the open field, or at the edge of the wood, where it has plenty of room, you will see that it has grown differently. The trunk is much larger, and the branches grow out lower down. In many big oaks a man can reach the lower boughs as he stands under it. The branches are very heavy and stretch out widely all round, so that an old oak tree covers a great deal of space in open ground. If the trunk were not very strong it could not bear the weight of such huge branches. But it is very broad at the bottom and then curves in and rises like a stout pillar till it becomes broad again where the branches divide away from it.

When Smeaton, the great engineer, built the Eddystone lighthouse, he shaped it like the trunk of an oak, and the lighthouse stood firm against wind and waves for more than a hundred years.

The oak has a very thick strong root from which long ropy roots run out all round the tree. I will tell you a way by which you may know how far the roots of a tree spread underground. Look at the branches and see how far they stretch out from the trunk, for the roots will reach just as far underground as the branches do above ground.

The reason of this is very interesting. You will remember that the tips of the roots are the mouths of a plant. They drink in the water. Now when it rains, the raindrops trickle from leaf to leaf till they come to the tips of the branches, and then they drip down and sink into the ground. The roots would get very little rain-water if they stopped under the tree where you and I stand to keep out of the rain. But as the tree grows, the roots find their way farther and farther out, till they reach the place where the drip will be.

You will find it useful to know this in gardening and farming, for tree roots are often very troublesome.

When you have looked at the rugged bark of the old oak, which is so useful for tanning leather, look up at the branches. They twist and turn in all directions, and there is a very thick joint wherever a new branch starts.

You can see the reason of this, if you look at your young tree, or at a twig of the old tree. There is not one bud at the tip of the twigs as there was in the horse-chestnut, but two, three, or sometimes more. All these buds crowd each other, and the middle one generally dies. The others go off different ways, and so make what carpenters call "knee-joints." These were used for shipbuilding in olden days, because they are very strong. But now that ships are made of iron, knee-timber is not so much wanted, and straight planks and poles are more valuable. So it is best now to plant oaks in woods, where their stems grow straight and smooth.

Oak timber has always been valuable. The beams of West-

OAK BRANCHES WITH ACORNS.
1. Common Oak with stalked Acorns.   *2.* Durmast Oak with
Acorns close to the branch.

CATKINS OF THE OAK.

minster Hall, which was built about nine hundred years ago, are made of Durmast Oak, and are still as good as ever. Many country cottages have old chests and carved chairs in them quite as old as this. The heartwood of the oak is very firm and strong, and this is why the old song says

> "Hearts of Oak are our ships,
> Hearts of Oak are our men."

You can see the trunk and branches of the oak best, in winter. Then when April is nearly over, a pretty crimson colour comes on all the buds, the leaves open out, and the loose catkins hang down between them, while the tiny acorn flowers nestle between the leaf-stalk and the stem.

When the leaves are fully out, and the acorns are beginning to form, try if you can find the two kinds of English oak. Their leaves are much the same shape, long and cut into deep divisions. But the leaves of the Common Oak have very short leaf-stalks, they almost touch the stem, while the acorns stand on long stalks. In the other tree called the Durmast Oak the leaves usually have longer stalks, and the acorns have none.

The evergreen oak, which is often grown in gardens, was brought from Italy. Its leaves are something like the leaves of the holly, so it is called the holm oak or holly oak.

Get a branch of oak and notice the crowded buds. Get a log of oak and notice the dark heartwood and the rings round it. Also the rugged bark. Try to find the two kinds of English oak. Notice the scales grown together in the acorn cup.

LESSON VI.
GUESTS OF THE OAK.

THE oak feeds more creatures than any other English tree. Not only do the pigs, the hedgehogs, the squirrels, and the field-mice feed on the acorns, but more than fifty kinds of insects get their food from some part of the tree.

Many of these are too small for you to find, but you will enjoy looking out for others. If you examine an oak-tree in May, you will most likely find some of its leaves rolled up, either from the tip towards the stalk, or from side to side. Undo this roll and you will find a caterpillar inside, or perhaps a chrysalis. There are two kinds of caterpillars which roll up oak leaves. One, which is called simply the Oak-moth caterpillar, is large. It rolls up the leaf rather untidily, and spins a cocoon round itself inside, in the shape of a little boat. The moth when it comes out has bright green wings with two white bands on them.

The other caterpillar, which you are almost sure to find, does its work more tidily. It makes a very neat roll, and fastens it together with fine threads. Then it feeds on the inner rolls till it goes to sleep, and turns into a moth. If you shake an oak-tree in June numbers of these little moths will often fly out. They are called the Green Oak-moth, though their hind wings are brown. They are much smaller than the oak-moth, whose caterpillar spins the boat cocoon.

Another insect which you may find, is the grub of the great Stag Beetle. For this you will have to cut into the trunks of old

trees, where the big grub hollows out a bed for itself under the bark. It stays there and feeds on the wood of the tree for three or four years, till it turns into the bee-

OAK LEAVES ROLLED UP WITH
CHRYSALIS INSIDE.

tle. You remember that the woodpecker taps with his beak as he climbs the trees. It is grubs like these that he is trying to find.

But the most curious homes on an oak-tree are the galls made by mother insects, which lay their eggs on some part of the tree. Every country child knows the red-brown rosy-cheeked oak-apple, which grows on the tips of the oak-twigs, and which many people mistake for fruit. Boys used to stick these in their hats on the twenty-ninth of May, because Charles the Second, who hid from his enemies in an oak-tree, came back to his throne on that day.

Instead of sticking it into your caps, cut the oak-apple

across with a sharp knife. You will find that it is soft and spongy, and is divided into a number of small cells. In each of these cells there will be either a grub, or a cocoon, or a perfect fly ready to come out. Or perhaps the home may be empty, all the inmates having flown away.

Let us see how this oak-apple came to be there. Early in the spring a small wasp-fly, called a Cynips, settled on the twig,

OAK-APPLE. INSECT CELLS SEEN IN THE APPLE CUT OPEN.

and pierced the bark with a sharp-pointed tube. She carries this tube coiled up at the end of her body, till she wants to use it. Then she darts it out into the twig and squeezes some juice into the hole, together with several eggs.

In a very short time a swelling rises up, and the spongy oak-apple grows round the eggs, each one being in a cell by itself. So when the grubs are hatched they find plenty of soft food to eat, till they spin their cocoons.

Another of these flies lays its eggs on the loose catkins. You may easily find them hanging like little brown currants on the stalk, after the flowers have withered. For though the stalk falls off as a rule, yet when these galls are on it, it remains hanging till the fly comes out.

These "currant galls" have each one grub in them, and so too have the galls which you will find under the leaves. There are at least two kinds of leaf-galls. One is bright red, and is called a "cherry gall." The other is very small, pink, hairy, and flat. There are a great many of these under each leaf, and they are called "oak-spangles". The grub remains in these galls after the leaves have fallen, so you will be able to find them.

The next gall I am sure you will think is a bud. It is called the "artichoke gall," and really begins in the oak-bud, in which the fly lays her eggs early in the spring. Then instead of grow-ing into a twig with green leaves, the bud covers itself with scales, and a number of grubs are hatched inside.

Last of all there are the big brown galls, specially called "oak-galls". They grow half-way down the twigs, and remain hanging on the tree all the winter, after the flies have flown out. This gall was first seen in England about sixty years ago, in 1840. It has spread very fast, and is hurtful to the trees, for it sucks out a great deal of sap. It is very like the galls which we get from Asia, in order to use the acid in them for making ink.

Many other trees have galls on them besides the oak, and I advise you when you find a curious lump or a strange-shaped bud, unlike anything you expect to find on a tree, to cut it open and see if there is a grub inside.

Find as many different kinds of oak-gall as you can. Find

the leaf-rolling caterpillars, and try to find the grub of the stag-beetle.

THE BEECH AND THE SWEET CHESTNUT.

As you go through the woods in spring, you should watch the trees when they break out into leaf. One of the prettiest is the Beech Tree, You may know it in the middle of winter by its olive-grey bark, its tall, smooth trunk with a broad crown of branches on the top, and its brown sharp-pointed buds which

OAK-GALLS.

1. Artichoke Galls.   *2.* Oak-spangles.   *3.* Currant Galls.
4. Hard brown Oak-gall.

I. BEECH TREE.   2. MAST OR BEECH NUT.
3. SWEET CHESTNUT.   4. NUTS IN THE HUSK.

grow one after the other, now on one side, now on the other of the stem. How different they are from the thick buds of the horse-chestnut, and yet they keep the little leaves inside quite as safe and warm.

Pick one of them to pieces in the early spring, just before they burst open. You will find, first, a number of shiny brown scales folded tight one over the other. Then inside these, some transparent scales as soft as silk, wrapping round the delicate tiny leaves which are folded up like a fan, and have a fringe of silvery hairs on them. Lastly, in the middle, the tender growing tip lies safely hidden.

A few days later these bright green leaves will open, and the scales hang loosely below them, while the silken fringe now shows as hairs under the leaves. Each leaf is oval and notched at the edge, and the twigs on which they grow droop at first, and then slowly raise themselves. By the time the leaves are full grown the brown clusters of flowers are hanging among them.

Those with the stamens in them are soft and silky, and hang on long, thin stalks; but those with the seed-boxes, stand up on short stalks near the end of the twigs. There are two or three of them on each stalk, with their sticky horns standing up, and a number of prickly scales round them.

These scales are like those we saw round the acorn. They grow into a hard husk covered with prickles, and by-and-by quite shut in the two or three little nuts. But when autumn comes, the "beech-mast", as it is called, falls down, the husk bursts open into four pieces, and then you see inside the three-cornered nuts with the withered horns still on the top.

Now, why do you think these scales grow into Such a hard

husk and shut in the fruit, and why do they burst in the autumn? Because the squirrels and field-mice feed chiefly on beech-nuts, and if there were no husk to protect the nuts while they are green, they would be eaten before they were ripe. But now the husk falls and bursts, just when they are ready to grow. The tree can spare a good many to be eaten, if the squir-

rels and other animals tread a few into the ground or bury there so that they grow. Beech trees spring up so well from seed that there is no need to plant them. But if you want to keep a beech wood healthy and cut it down for timber you must take care of it. The trees live for more than two hundred years, though they are ready to be cut down when they are about ninety years old.

Good foresters cut down one block at a time, so that there is always some part of the wood getting ready for timber. In the part they are going to cut, they first clear away the

BEECH BUDS IN WINTER.
The top Bud is stripped of it's brown Scales.

other kinds of trees and the young stunted beeches, so as to let in the light and air.

Then they wait for a year or two, till there comes a season when the beech-mast is good, and the seeds are strong and will grow well. This happens generally about every three or four years. Then they begin to thin out the trees for timber, and so to leave room for young seedlings to grow up and begin a new crop.

After this they go on cutting down some every year, and clear that piece of the wood in about ten years or more. By that time the new beech-trees have a good crown of branches and leaves on the top and go on and grow, while the forester begins to cut down another part of the wood.

If the beech-tree is pretty in spring, it is still more lovely in the autumn, when its leaves turn a bright red, and by-and-by fall and make a lovely carpet of leaves in the wood. The young beech-trees keep their dead leaves on all through the winter, and so do beech-hedges, which are kept cut and not allowed to grow into trees.

There is another tree you know well, which shuts up its fruit in a husk made of prickly scales. This is the sweet or Spanish chestnut, which the Romans brought to our country, and which now grows in the woods, or is often planted in the avenues leading to big houses. It opens its leaves later than the beech, and does not bloom till July. Still by October the nuts are ripe, and the husks burst open on the ground. And when you pick up the nuts to take them home to roast, you may notice the dry remains of the flower making a kind of bristling fringe on their points. Quite late in the autumn the chestnut is a lovely tree. Its long narrow leaves, cut in sharp points at the edge turn a beautiful golden brown and hang on a long time.

Many beams of old houses are made of chestnut, and the trunks of the young trees are made into hop-poles. Beech-wood is used very largely for making chairs.

The Birch and the Alder are both trees with catkins and

hard-shelled fruits like the beech and the oak. They flower in the early spring before the leaves are fully out. The alder grows near streams or on wet ground. The birch you will find in the woods, and know it by its slender, graceful trunk, marked with brown, yellow and silvery streaks, its purple-brown twigs, and its dark green leaves—these smell very strong after rain, because the resin oozes from them. Some diseased birches have large tufts of twigs growing on the upper branches, looking like crows' nests.

Bring, in spring, a beech branch with its buds. Bring, in autumn, beech-nuts and chestnuts in their husks. Compare a chestnut, which is a fruit, with a horse chestnut, which is a seed. Find Birch and Alder fruits.

LESSON VIII.

TREES WHICH BEAR CONES.

PINES, firs, and larches grow in almost all parts of England. They are very interesting and useful trees. They all form their seeds in woody cones, and their leaves are very narrow or needle-shaped, quite unlike the leaves of most other trees.

A large part of the timber we use comes from pines and firs, grown in Norway and other countries. It is called pine-wood and deal. No doubt you have noticed the small round pieces called "knots" in deal, and have poked them out, leaving a hole. These are places where branches grew and broke off, and then the trunk closed round them; they are common in deal and pinewood. The sap in these trees is very resinous and they are tapped for turpentine. If you walk in a pine wood, or crush the leaves of a pine or fir, you will notice the strong scent of this resinous juice.

Every country child has picked up fir cones, and you may easily find three different kinds, those belonging to the Scotch pine, the Spruce fir, and the Larch. Of these three, only the Scotch pine is a native of Great Britain, the other two have been brought from abroad.

There were once dense forests of Scotch pine in England, but these have been cut down long ago, and the pine woods we have now, have grown up from the seeds of trees brought from the great forests in Scotland, Norway, and France. It is a tall tree with spreading branches and a trunk covered with a red or brown scaly bark. Perhaps you know it as Scotch fir, for people confuse these two names, and call the same tree "pine" or "fir," though you may know the difference if you look at the cones.

The dark-green leaves of the Scotch pine are very narrow, and about two inches long (see coloured plate). They grow two together in a sheath of brown scales. Its cones have no stalks, and they bulge out at the bottom, and taper away to a blunt point at the upper end. They are made of a number of thick woody scales which look as if they were folded back at the top, making a solid thick knob with a brown scaly spot where the tip ends. These scales fit over each other so tightly that, before the cone is ripe, not even a drop of rain can get in, and they take two or three years to ripen. Sometimes they hang all the time on the tree. Sometimes they fall off earlier. As they ripen, the woody scales bend outwards and you can see two thin, transparent scales inside each, which look like the wings of a fly. They stand upright against the woody scale.

I. SCOTCH PINE AND CONES. 2. SPRUCE FIR AND CONES.

Slip a knife carefully down under these, right to the bottom and pull them out. You will find a seed at the end of each, if you have not broken the tender translucent membrane.

For these are winged seeds, which have no seed-box over them, but grow naked inside the woody scale. After a time they fall out and are blown away by the wind. If you get a cone that is too old they will be gone.

All trees with cones have these winged seeds, and the cones of true pines are very much alike. You will easily know the Cluster pine,

**LARCH TWIG
BEARING CONES.**

which has been brought from France and is found in many English woods among the Scotch pines. Its large cones grow in clusters round the branches, four or sometimes eight, together. They are larger and browner than the cones of the Scotch pine and they often remain a great many years on the tree.

The Spruce fir is very different from the Scotch pine. Its spreading branches grow nearly down to the ground, and its needle-shaped leaves, which are barely an inch long grow singly on the stem. Its cones are long and narrow and the scales are not so thick as in pines. But the chief difference is that the tips are not bent back into knobs, they are pointed and bend in a little, and by this you may know fir-cones from pine-cones.

The firs have two seeds inside each scale like the pine, but these ripen in one year. The spruce fir came from Norway, and now grows all over England.

The Larch, which came from Switzerland, and the Cedar, which came from Lebanon in Palestine, both grow their seeds in cones, but they are rather different from the pines and firs. Their needle-leaves are very thin and grow in tufts eighteen or twenty together in the same sheath of scales. The cones of the cedar stand upright and are shaped like an egg, but the tree does not often bear cones in England.

TWIGS OF YEW.
1. With Flowers in Spring.
2. With red Cup and Seed in Autumn.

Larch cones are quite small, not more than an inch in length; they grow along the twigs in a row. The woody scales do not fit very tightly together.

I think you can find the cones of all these trees except the cedar. Of course you must look for fir and larch cones in the autumn, because they ripen each year, but pine-cones are on the trees all the year round. If you look at any of these trees in the spring and early summer, you will see their stamen-catkins hanging from the branches, and the yellow pollen blowing about in clouds so as to fall on the young cones.

Pines, firs, and cedars are evergreen trees. Their leaves remain on the tree three years or more; and as the branches are not of the same age, the leaves fall off in different years, so that the trees are always green. But the larch sheds its leaves every year, and you may easily know it, in the autumn by its bare drooping boughs covered with small brown cones.

Pines and firs will flourish in very poor soil and their seeds grow up easily. If you are near a pine wood, or a wood of mixed trees with pines or firs in it, try and find a seedling tree. It is curious to look at, for it shoots up with a long, thin stalk, and carries up the seed-coat with it. When this coat falls off, you see five or six long seed-leaves underneath, and in the middle of them a bud with the real pine or fir leaves.

There is another tree which you know well, which has needle-shaped leaves. They grow all round the stem, two together in each sheath, but they are flattened down on two sides of the stem like the featherlets of a feather. This is the Yew tree, which you find so often in church-yards. It does not bear cones. Its naked seeds sit each one in a red juicy cup. The stamen-catkins are not on the same tree as the red cups, but if you search well you will find them on another yew tree.

Bring in a bunch of the Scotch pine and the Spruce fir. Compare the cones of the two trees. Try to find a branch of Cedar, a branch of the Larch with cones, a seedling pine or fir, a branch of Yew with stamen flowers in March, and another with the red cup and naked seed in the autumn.

LESSON IX.

HEDGEROW SHRUBS AND TREES.

THERE is no country in the world where the hedge-rows are so beautiful as in England. Whether we look at the neatly trimmed hedges round our gardens, or the roughly-trimmed fences between the fields, they each have their beauty. Perhaps the most delightful of all, to look at, are the hedges which are not cut more than once in six years. But these are not good for the fields.

Let us look first at the garden hedges. Have you ever thought that these are all made of young trees, clipped so that they remain only branches and leaves, and do not grow tall trunks? A box hedge is made of box trees closely cut. The holly hedge, whose prickly leaves are so useful in preventing the cattle from breaking through, would grow into tall trees if left alone. I know a garden in Devonshire where there are holly trees thirty feet high, growing here and there in a holly hedge.

The hawthorn fence is the same as the May-tree which grows on the lawn. The beech hedge is made of beech trees, kept well clipped, and the dead leaves hang on it in winter, as they do on young beeches. The yew hedge is the same as the big yew tree in the churchyard, and it is well to be careful how you plant it anywhere near cattle and horses, for in a hard winter they sometimes eat the poisonous leaves and die.

But each of these hedges is made of only one kind of tree. They are not nearly so interesting as the mixed hedges which grow between the fields. There we find blackberries and nuts and all sorts of curious fruits and flowers.

Do you know the Blackthorn bush, whose small white

flowers grow on its black stem, almost before winter is over and while it has no leaves? If you do, I expect you know that you will find purple sloes on it in the autumn, under its small dark-green leaves, and you can gather the fruit to make sloe syrup or sloe wine. The blackthorn is not a good hedge plant, for its roots wander far out into the field, and it often grows into a tree and so leaves a gap in the fence.

The Hawthorn or May is much better, for it grows into a thick quickset hedge, if it is properly cut, and the cattle do not break through it, because of its thorns. But you cannot use the fruit of the hawthorn, you must leave the haws for the birds.

Then, in the hedge, or the wood, you will most likely find the Crab-apple tree, with its spreading branches, often covered with thorns. It has oval leaves with sharp points, which are downy underneath when they are young. Its rosy pink-and-white blossoms come out in May, and in the autumn you will find the red crab-apple in their place. This fruit is sour and bitter.

Another hedgerow tree is the Wild Cherry, whose fruit feeds the birds in the summer, and helps to keep them away from the corn. It is a bushy shrub with a red bark and blue-green egg-shaped leaves, very much notched round the edge. Its flowers grow on short stalks four or five from one point like our garden cherries, and the fruit, when it is ripe, is a bright red. If you live in Wales, or the middle or north of England, you may find another tree called the Bird-cherry, whose flowers grow along a thin stalk, and its fruit is black. But be sure you find the right one with long, drooping flower clusters, for many people call the wild dwarf cherry by this name.

The blackthorn, hawthorn, crab-apple, and cherry all belong to the rose family, which, you remember, has so many
fruit-bearing plants in it. So does the pretty Rowan tree, often
called the Mountain Ash, because its leaves are cut into leaflets
very like those of the ash-tree. You will find the small white
flowers of the Rowan tree open in May. But you will like it best

I. BIRD CHERRY.   2. GUELDER ROSE.

in autumn when the clusters of beautiful red berries are ripe.
Perhaps you have one over your gate, for they were often
planted there when people believed in witches, as they were
supposed to keep them away.

I must find room to tell you of two more hedgerow shrubs.
One is the Guelder Rose, which has dark-green leaves cut into

1. ROWAN TREE.   2. SPINDLE TREE.

three or five points with a jagged edge. These leaves turn a lovely red in the autumn. Its white flowers grow in a flat cluster. The outer ones are large and have neither stamens nor seed-box in them. Their use is to attract the bees and flies, which come to the smaller flowers in the middle to fetch honey. These middle flowers are perfect and so the insects help them to form seed. The guelder rose has beautiful coral-red berries in the autumn.

The other bush, which grows about five feet high in the hedge, is called the Spindle tree, because its wood is used for making spindles and skewers. It has a smooth, grey stem and narrow, green leaves, which are very poisonous. You will scarcely notice its small green-white flowers in May. But in the autumn it has a lovely and curious fruit. Four red seed-boxes grow together in a clump on a short stalk. They look very quaint, and if you open them you will find that the seed inside is covered with a bright orange-coloured membrane.

Find the flowers and fruit of the blackthorn, may, apple and wild cherry, rowan tree, guelder rose, and spindle tree.

LESSON X.
GARDEN SHRUBS IN BLOOM.

THERE is not room to grow large trees in a cottage garden, but many flowering shrubs can be planted in corners, and some of them are very lovely. The first to bloom in the year is the Japan pear, Pyrus japonica. It grows on many cottage walls, and makes them bright when the trees are bare of leaves. Its deep-red buds are showing even in January, and by the end of February the wall is covered with them. They are like pear blossoms in shape, and grow in little bunches close against the stem. If you have not got one you will easily find a sucker, growing out from some neighbour's plant, and it is not difficult to rear. In the autumn you will see its hard, green fruit.

Soon after the Japan pear is in full bloom the *Ribes*, or "flowering currant," will be showing its red tassels in most gardens. It was first brought from North America, and has spread all over England. You will easily know it, because its leaves are very like those of the currant-bushes in the kitchen garden, and its pretty hanging

THE WILD BARBERRY.

clusters of red or pink flowers are shaped like the little green blossoms of our currants and gooseberries. Then in the autumn it has hanging bunches of dark berries, which are not good to eat. A piece of Ribes cut off and stuck in the ground will grow without any trouble.

Another very pretty bush flowers in early summer. This is the Barberry, whose small scarlet fruits used at one time to be put inside sugar plums. The barberry is an interesting shrub, for it has turned some of its leaves into thorns, so that at each joint there is a three-pronged thorn, as well as the smooth, fringed leaves. The wild barberry has yellow flowers with bright red anthers, but there is a garden kind with ever-green leaves, which has deep orange-coloured flowers. They are small and hang in a long spray, and if you are clever you can try an experiment with either the wild or garden barberry.

Look carefully at one of the flowers and you will see that the six stamens are spread out, one lying down upon each petal. At the bottom of the petal, near the middle of the flower, are two bags, out of which oozes honey in drops. The sticky stigma on the top of the seed-box stands up in the middle of the flower.

Now take a needle and touch one of the stamens at its base, just where the honey drops are. It will jump up, as if moved by a spring, and touch the sticky stigma, then after a little while it will fall down again. Now when a bee puts her head in for honey she irritates the stamen so that it jumps up and hits her and she carries the pollen-dust to another flower. Or the anther leaves some pollen on its own stigma, before it falls down again.

But we must go on, for when the "March winds and April showers bring forth May flowers" there will be plenty of shrubs to look at. There is the Spanish Broom, with its bright yellow blossoms shaped like a pea-flower. You can find wild broom growing on the heaths. It is very like gorse, only it has smooth, green stems, and no prickles. But in the wild broom the blossoms grow singly on the stem, while in Spanish broom they form bright yellow clusters. The broom has no honey, but the bees come to it for pollen-dust to make bee-bread.

RED FLOWER, JAPAN PEAR.
WHITE FLOWER, SNOWBALL TREE.

If there is a Lilac bush growing near the broom you will notice how lovely the two colours, yellow and lilac, look together. You can make a very pretty nosegay from the two shrubs. But you will make a more graceful one, if you can find a Laburnum with its long sprays of golden blossom. The laburnum has plenty of honey in its flowers, and, as the bees have to gnaw a lump to get at it, they often stop a long time at each flower, and you may see many on one tree. Laburnum pods are like small pea-pods, but take care not to eat the seeds in them, for they are very poisonous.

Next the Rhododendrons will be opening their beautiful bunches of red-purple flowers among their glossy, green leaves. These come from North America. But the Elderbush, which grows in the corner, making a pleasant shade over a little seat, is a true English shrub, which almost deserves to be called a tree. It does not bloom much before July, but it is one of the first trees to put out its leaves in the early spring. Though it is not tall, it has very thick stems, and its bark is rough and corky.

You must take the young branches if you want to make pop-guns, for in the old ones the pith is crushed up into quite a tiny space by the rings of wood outside. The leaves of the elder grow opposite to each other on the stem, and each leaf is cut into seven or nine leaflets, with one at the end. The small white flowers grow in very large flat clusters, and leave the sweet elder-berries behind them in the autumn.

If you have not an elder tree in the garden, you will very likely have a Snowball tree. This is a garden kind of Guelder rose. Its blossoms are not in a flat bunch as they are on the wild tree. They grow in a ball and they have no stamens or seedbox in them, so they make no seeds. But the leaves turn purple in the autumn and are very lovely.

By this time the big purple Clematis will be out over the porch. It will last in bloom till October, and behind it on the wall grows the Myrtle, which will be covered with white flowers in August. We all know the myrtle so well that it is difficult to believe that it is not a British shrub. It came from the south of France, and now grows in all warm parts of England, keeping our walls green all the year round. Its oval leaves give a delightful scent from the little pockets of oil, which you may see if you look through the leaf at the light.

Bring flowers and leaves of any of the shrubs mentioned.

LESSON XI.
THE ASH AND THE ELM.

NEXT to the oak, the two hardwood trees which are most useful are the ash and the elm. Both these trees grow in the hedgerows as well as in the open fields, and they both blossom quite early in the year, before they put forth their leaves.

You may know Ash stems anywhere, even in winter, by two things. First by the tips of its branches, which are flat, as if they had been pressed under a weight. And secondly by its black buds shaped like little pyramids. No other tree has black buds like these. The trunk is an ash-grey colour, and the branches grow very gracefully, first dipping down from the boughs and then tilting up again like the horns of a deer.

In April the ash-buds on the side branches near to the tip begin to open out into clusters of purple-black flowers (2). Each flower is very small. It has no flower-leaves, nothing but a seed-box and two purple stamens. But these tiny flowers are so closely crowded that the whole tree is coloured by them.

Then, at the end of May, the leaf-buds begin to open. The leaves grow opposite to each other on the branches, and each leaf (1) is cut into seven or more leaflets, with an odd one at the end. Many leaves are cut up like this, and you might think each leaflet was a leaf. But if they were leaves, a bud would grow at the base of each, near the stem, and there would be a growing tip at the end. So when there are neither of these you may know that all the leaflets make up one leaf; and when it fades, the whole falls off together.

All through the summer the tree is very beautiful, and its bluish-grey leaves differ from those of any other tree. But early in the autumn they turn yellow and fall. Then you will know the tree by its curious long, flat, narrow fruits (3), which hang in groups from the branches like bunches of keys. In fact, they are called "keys." They hang on sometimes quite into the winter, till the rough winds tear them off.

You may often find a young ash-tree growing in your garden, for they are very hardy. But rabbits are fond of eating the young seedlings, so they have not much chance to grow. Young ash stems are often used for walking-sticks and hop-poles, and the wood, when full-grown, sells very well for coach-building and for making furniture.

We all know Elm-trees so well that perhaps you may think that there is nothing interesting to learn about them. But I wonder if you have noticed that the twigs of an elm grow on the trunk almost to the bottom of the tree unless they are lopped off. And I am almost sure that many of you do not know that the twigs are often covered with little lumps of cork, making the branch look as if it were diseased.

Next to the oak, the two hardwood trees which are most useful are the ash and the elm. Both these trees grow in the hedgerows as well as in the open fields, and they both blossom quite early in the year, before they put forth their leaves.

TIP OF A BRANCH OF ASH.
1. Leaf of nine Leaflets.
2. Flowers.
3. Fruit, called "Keys."

You may know Ash stems anywhere, even in winter, by two things. First by the tips of its branches, which are flat, as if they had been pressed under a weight. And secondly by its black buds shaped like little pyramids. No other tree has black buds like these. The trunk is an ash-grey colour, and the branches grow very gracefully, first dipping down from the boughs and then tilting up again like the horns of a deer.

In April the ash-buds on the side branches near to the tip begin to open out into clusters of purple-black flowers (2). Each flower is very small. It has no flower-leaves, nothing but a seed-box and two purple stamens. But these tiny flowers are so closely crowded that the whole tree is coloured by them.

Then, at the end of May, the leaf-buds begin to open. The leaves grow opposite to each other on the branches, and each leaf (1) is cut into seven or more leaflets, with an odd one at the end. Many leaves are cut up like this, and you might think each leaflet was a leaf. But if they were leaves, a bud would grow at the base of each, near the stem, and there would be a growing tip at the end. So when there are neither of these you may know that all the leaflets make up one leaf; and when it fades, the whole falls off together.

All through the summer the tree is very beautiful, and its bluish-grey leaves differ from those of any other tree. But early in the autumn they turn yellow and fall. Then you will know the tree by its curious long, flat, narrow fruits (3), which hang in groups from the branches like bunches of keys. In fact, they are called "keys." They hang on sometimes quite into the winter, till the rough winds tear them off.

You may often find a young ash-tree growing in your garden, for they are very hardy. But rabbits are fond of eating the young seedlings, so they have not much chance to grow. Young ash stems are often used for walking-sticks and hop-poles, and the wood, when full-grown, sells very well for coach-building and for making furniture.

We all know Elm-trees so well that perhaps you may think that there is nothing interesting to learn about them. But I wonder if you have noticed that the twigs of an elm grow on the trunk almost to the bottom of the tree unless they are lopped off. And I am almost sure that many of you do not know that the twigs are often covered with little lumps of cork, making the branch look as if it were diseased.

It is really quite healthy, but it tells a secret, namely, that the elm has a very corky bark. Even on the trunk the cork is thick and rugged, and on the small branches it has no room to spread, and has to lie in lumps. The inner part of the bark called the "liber" is very tough, and is used for making mats and ropes.

The common elm, which so often grows in rows between the fields, or is planted on the village green, was brought to England by the Romans. It is not quite at home even now, for its seeds do not ripen, except in very hot summers, and new trees have to be planted from suckers.

TWIG OF ELM-TREE COVERED WITH CORK.

The real old elm of England is the Wych elm or Scotch elm. It has not such a tall trunk as the common elm, for its big branches grow out much lower down. Its leaves are bigger, and its seeds ripen and grow, when they are sown. But it is not very common in our country and grows chiefly in Scotland, Wales, and the West of England.

Even in winter you can count a great number of buds on

the elm, and when April comes, if you look up through the boughs, you will see a purple tinge all over the top of the tree. This is caused by the tiny purple flowers which burst out on the twigs. Now watch the tree. At the end of April the fresh green leaves peep out of the leaf-buds. But already the seed-boxes are beginning to fall and are blown into heaps by the wind.

ELM-TREE TWIGS
1. Twigs with Flowers.   2. Twig with Ovaries.

I am sure you must know these little, flat, green plates, with a lump in the middle where the seed lies. They are blown along the fields, and often down the village street, filling the gutters.

If they fall from the Common elm it is very doubtful whether they will grow. But if you have a Wych elm on the green, you may know its seed-boxes, because the seed always lies quite in the middle of the plate, while in the common elm it lies nearer the point. These seeds are ripe and worth sowing.

There are a great many kinds of elm in England, very like each other, but it is easy to know the Cornish elm because it grows such a great deal of cork on its twigs. All the big forest elms are very useful for timber. They sometimes live for four or five hundred years, but the best time for cutting them down is when they are about one hundred and twenty years old.

A great many insects feed on the elm. The most destructive one is a beetle which eats its way down to the inner bark, and sucks the sap. Then the mother beetle works her way down about two inches and makes little galleries all along the tube on each side. In each gallery she lays an egg, and the grubs when they are hatched eat the wood. The trees of whole forests have been killed by this "elm-destroying beetle."

Bring an ash branch to look at the twigs and buds. Find a bunch of ash-keys. Find the corky twigs of the elm, and the green seed-plates in May. Look in decayed elms for the galleries of the elm-destroying beetle.

LESSON XII.
IN THE PARK.

IN our great parks you will find the largest and grandest English trees, besides many which are interesting because they come from abroad. Avenues, of a mile or two miles long, are often planted with one kind of tree, chestnut, beech, oak, horse-chestnut, or lime, while in the open ground the oaks and horse-chestnuts grow into much finer trees than in the fields.

We have not yet spoken of the Lime-tree, but you know it quite well, with its straight, smooth trunk, its bright, heart-shaped green leaves, bigger on one side than the other, and pointed at the tip, and its bunches of yellowish green flowers, which grow on a long stalk coming out of the middle of a yel-low-green leaf.

Get some of these flowers in July, or some of the round, downy fruit with ribs on it in the autumn when it is ripe. The leaf out of which they grow is called a bract, and is the same kind of leaf as the scales on which the willow stamens, and the pine seeds grow. But in the Lime it has become a long leaf which can be carried by the wind. The inner bark or "liber" of the lime tree is very useful in making ropes, and of all trees the bees love this one, for the flowers have a sweet scent and plenty of honey in their cups.

There is another tree, which is almost as useful to the bees, which blooms rather earlier than the lime. This is the Sycamore, whose clusters of green flowers hang from the twigs in May, before the leaves are quite out. The sycamore is a very handsome tree with large leaves cut into five broad divisions. It is really a kind of maple, very like the common English field maple which grows in the hedges. If you stand under a sycamore in warm weather you will often notice that drops fall from it, and you will find that its leaves are sticky. This is be-cause all maples have a great deal of very sugary juice or sap in them, which rises up and oozes out of the leaves, either from cracks made by the leaf being dry, or because some insect has bitten a hole. You must have seen the little green blight-insects

1. ARBUTUS, OR STRAWBERRY TREE, IN FLOWER AND FRUIT.
2. LIME TREE IN FLOWER.

which cling on rose trees and other plants, and suck out their juice. Hundreds and thousands of these, besides other bugs (such as the cuckoo-spit, which you find covered with froth), suck the sap of trees. So through the cracks they have made the sugary juice of the sycamore or the maple oozes out over the leaves.

The fruit of these trees is very curious. It is winged like the keys of the ash, but two fruits grow together, so that the two wings spread out like those of a moth. The wings of the Field Maple fruit are spread more widely than those of the sycamore.

Maple wood is very useful for fur-niture. A great many of our desks and wardrobes are made from American maple. Maple sugar, which American children love, comes from the sugary sap of an American species.

SYCAMORE TWIG
WITH IT'S FRUIT.

Another tree which you will find in the park is the Walnut, which was brought to England by the Romans. It is a large, spreading tree with a rough trunk and strong, crooked branches. Its leaves are cut like those of the ash, but they are much larger. They have a pretty red tinge when they are young, and always have a strong smell when they are crushed.

These trees grow so quickly that they are twenty feet high in ten years, and then begin to flower and make fruit. They go on growing till they are about seventy feet high. You can see the long catkins hanging from the tree in April just as the leaves are opening. The stamen catkins are at the tip of last year's twigs. But the little group of flowers which will grow into walnuts are on the new twigs, which have just come from buds. In autumn every boy knows the walnut fruit shut up in the green husk, which stains your fingers brown as you peel it off. When the husk is off you can slip a knife between the halves of the hard shell and split them apart. In doing this you divide the two seed-leaves of the seed, which are the parts you eat; and if you look carefully you will see the little white bud and root, lying between them, at the pointed end of the walnut. Walnut wood is very useful for furniture, for it becomes a deep brown when the tree is old, and has very beautiful veins in it.

There is one more tree or shrub which grows only in parks and shrubberies, about which I must tell you, because it is so pretty. But I am not sure you will be able to find one. It is the Arbutus, or Strawberry tree so called because its fruits look like strawberries. It is an evergreen shrub with green, glossy leaves shaped like a bay leaf and very notched at the edge. Its flowers are bell-shaped and waxy like the flowers of the heath, and they hang on bent stalks. But the curious thing about them is, that the fruits take a year to ripen. First they are a pale yellow, then they grow deeper and deeper in colour till they are a bright scarlet, hanging in twos and threes among the dark-green leaves, just when the tree blooms afresh with its pretty, greenish-white flowers.

Other trees which you may find in the park are the Chili pine, or monkey-puzzle, a tree which bears cones and has such prickly leaves close together, that it would indeed puzzle a monkey to climb it, and the large magnolias and tulip-trees which have such beautiful white and pinkish flowers as large as bowls. But these are foreigners and we must be content with knowing about English-growing trees.

Find the flowers and fruit of the lime tree; the leaves of the sycamore sticky with honey-dew; the winged seeds of the maple and the sycamore; the leaves and catkins of the walnut tree. Open a walnut and find the young shoot inside.

LESSON XIII.
LEAVES—THEIR SHAPE AND POSITION.

In the summer when the trees are in full leaf, and you have learnt to know them, you should bring in leafy twigs from each tree and note how the leaves grow on the stem, and what shapes they have.

We have already noticed that some trees, such as the horse-chestnut and the maple, have their leaves opposite to each other on the stem, two growing on each joint, while others, such as the elm and the beech for example, have their leaves alternate, one only growing from each joint. But there are many kinds of alternate leaves, and you will enjoy finding them out.

In the elm and the beech every *other leaf* comes exactly above the one below. Leaf 1 comes on one side of the stem, leaf 2 on the other side, leaf 3 exactly above leaf 1. But if you take a twig of the trembling poplar, or Aspen, it will be leaf 4 which comes above leaf 1. They have crept more slowly round the stem. Then take a twig of oak. You will find that you will have to count six leaves before you find one exactly over the first one. All these differences have their use, and when you are in the lanes, if you look at the trees, you will see how these arrangements bring the leaves into positions where they can best get light and air.

The next thing to look at is the shape of the leaves themselves. Botanists have a great many names to describe the shapes, the edges, the veins, and the divisions of leaves. I can only tell you of a few, so that you may keep your eyes open and notice others.

Leaves which are whole, so that you cannot pull off one piece without tearing it away from the rest, are called *simple*. The leaves of the elm, beech, sweet-chestnut, lime, oak, willow, sycamore, and many others are *simple*.

Leaves which are cut into separate leaflets, so that you can pull one off without touching the others, are called *compound*. The leaves of the horse-chestnut, ash, rose, rowan-tree, and elder are *compound*. You will remember that you know the divisions are leaflets and not leaves, because there is no growing tip at the end, and there are no buds in the angles. The leaflets grow out from the top of the leaf stalk (horse-chestnut), or from the narrow, green line, up the middle (rose), which is not a stalk, but the midrib of the leaf.

Now take all the simple leaves you have, and see what shapes they are. The best way to find out this is to lay a leaf on your slate and draw a line round it. This is very easy with a beech leaf, or the leaf of a sweet-chestnut. But when you take an oak leaf, you will want to know whether you are to run in and out of the divisions.

For the *shape* of a leaf you are not to do this. You are to begin at the leaf stalk and run round the *outside* points of the leaf all the way till you come back to the leaf stalk again. If you go round a maple leaf like this you will have a shape something like a *kidney*. A sycamore leaf will be more *heart-shaped*, longer, and ending in a blunt tip. An oak leaf will be *oblong*, longer than it is broad. The leaf of an elm or a beech you will

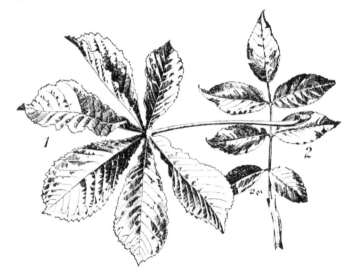

TIP OF A BRANCH OF ASH.
1. Horse Chestnut.   2. Rose.

find is shaped like an *egg*, and so is called oval, while the leaf of the sweet-chestnut is narrow and long. Lastly, if you take a lime leaf it will be heart-shaped, but uneven, one side of the leaf larger than the other. It is called *oblique*.

Now let us see how much the different leaves are cut. Some, like those of the lilac and ivy, are smooth at the edge. Others are *wavy*, and the holly has prickles at the end of its waves to

SHAPES AND EDGES OF LEAVES.

1. Beech–*oval, edge wavy.*   2. Oak–*oblong, deeply wavy.*
3. Sweet Chestnut–*narrow, broadly sawed.*   4. Birch–
doubly sawed.   5. Lime–*hear shaped and oblque.*
6. Sycamore–*hear-shaped, five lobed.* 7. Maple–*kidney-shaped, five lobed.*

protect it. But, if you look at holly leaves near the top of a tree where the cattle cannot reach, you will often find they do not take the trouble to grow prickles.

Other leaves have *teeth* round the edge. The leaf of the sweet-chestnut is toothed like a *saw*. So is a birch leaf, but if you look closely you will find it has two sets of teeth. The large teeth have their edges cut into small teeth. This leaf has a *double-sawed* edge. Some leaves again are very deeply cut into divisions or lobes. An oak leaf is cut, sometimes only in a wavy line, and sometimes into quite large divisions. A sycamore leaf has five large pointed divisions or *lobes*.

Get these two leaves and compare them. You will see that the veins which make the skeleton of the different shapes are not the same. In the sycamore leaf the large veins, or ribs, start from the top of the stalk, and spread out like five fingers, while the little veins start out from them. A leaf like this is called a palm-veined or *palmate-veined* leaf because the veins are like fingers on a hand. In the oak leaf, on the contrary, one long rib runs up the middle. The smaller ones start from it, like the featherlets of a bird's feather. So an oak leaf is said to be feather-veined or *pinnate-veined*, from *pinna*, a feather.

Now take the *compound* leaves of the horse-chestnut, ash, and rose. In the horse-chestnut the *leaflets* grow just like the veins of the sycamore. Seven fingers start from the top of the leaf stalk and spread out like fingers, so it is called a *palmate* leaf. But the ash and the rose have a rib up the middle and the separate leaflets are arranged feather-wise. So these leaves are called *pinnate*.

There are a great many leaves with shapes between these,

and if you collect them and arrange them in an old copy book, you will soon get an idea of the meaning of their names.

Describe the leaves of the oak, horse-chestnut, and elm and their position on the stem. Arrange any simple leaves and compound leaves you can find in a copy book and describe them.

BOOK VI
INSECT LIFE

"EYES AND NO EYES"

Sixth Book.

INSECT LIFE.

LESSON I.

WHAT IS AN INSECT?

IT is a lovely summer morning. Let us shut up our books and wander in the garden and field, in search of insects. The best way is to take a few card match-boxes with us, and drop one insect into each as we find them. Then when we get back to school, we can put them separately under tumblers.

Insects are so small that we often pass them by. But they form three-fourths of the whole animal kingdom, and they do us so much good and so much harm that we ought to know about them.

As we start I see a Cabbage Butterfly in the kitchen garden, and a beautiful Red Admiral flitting about among the flowers. We will take the Cabbage Butterfly, so that she may not lay her eggs on our cabbages.

Next stop at this rose-tree, there are a number of tiny insects, on the flower-stalks. If you look closely, you will see that each one has his beak buried in the stem, so as to suck out the juice. These are plant-lice. Each one is called an Aphis, and in the plural they are called Aphides.

We must syringe the tree with soft soap and tobacco water, or it will soon be covered with these insects, for they increase at the rate of more than a million in a month, and they stick out all the sweet sap from the plants to which they cling. On the same tree you will very likely find a Lady-bird, for she feeds on aphides.

Now look into the flower of this old Cabbage Rose, which grows in most cottage gardens. You are almost sure to find in it a lovely Rose-beetle with green shining wings shot with gold. Take it up and look at the bright wing-cases. While you are looking, it may open these cases and spread out the transparent wings underneath; but if it flies away you can easily get another.

Now, look! At your feet runs a beetle which is not half so pretty. It is the Cocktail, or Rove Beetle, often called the Devil's Coach-horse. As you pick him up he will cock up his tail and squirt out a very disagreeable fluid over your fingers, while he raises his head and snaps with his jaws. So drop him in his box quickly. The fact, is, he is terribly frightened, and hopes to make you set him free.

Now we will go out into the newly-mown field, and there you will see a number of small green Grasshoppers hopping about. They have been hatched under the earth-clods, and are eating the tips of the young grass. Some will have wings, but others, which are not fully grown, will have none. Pick one up and make him too a prisoner.

Next try to find a Wasp or a Bee. You can pick it up in your handkerchief and drop it in its box. We must go down to the river to find a May-fly or a Dragon-fly, and near there we shall easily get a Daddy-long-legs. But if there is not one to be seen,

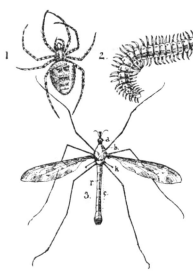

1. SPIDER.   2. CENTIPEDE
3. DADDY-LONG-LEGS.
k. Knobs or balancers.

a Blue-bottle or a Gnat will do.

You will wonder that I have not asked for a Spider. You had better get one, and also a Hundred-legs or Centipede, if you can find it.

When you have put these specimens under their glasses, look carefully at them. You will find a difference between the spider, the hundred-legs and all the others. The spider has eight legs and the centipede a very great many, while all the others have only six.

Now look at the Grasshopper, the Wasp, and the Daddy-long-legs. You will see very clearly that their bodies are divided into three parts—(a) the head; (b) the front body, on which the six legs and the wings grow; (c) the hind body, which has no legs on it, even when it is very long, as in the daddy-long-legs and the May-fly. You cannot see these divisions quite so well in the beetle because its wing-cases cover the join between the front and hind body.

We had better call these three divisions by their right names—(a) head; (b) front body, or, thorax; (c) hind body, or, abdomen. It is because insects are cut into these three parts that they have their name. It comes from the Latin "inseco" (I cut into). The Spider's head is not clearly divided from its

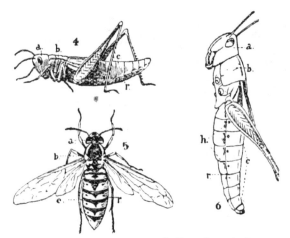

4&6. GRASSHOPPERS. *h*. Breathing holes.
5. WASP. *r*. Rings. *a*. Head. *b*. Thorax
c. Abdomen.

body, and a Centipede has not three divisions. For this reason, and because they have not six legs, some naturalists separate them from the true insects. This is why I did not call them insects.

Another thing you can notice well in the little green Grasshopper: his body is divided into rings (r), from his tail up to his head; and you can see the same in the wasp and the daddy-long-legs, the aphis and the cocktail beetle. All insects have ringed bodies.

It is these rings which enable the Wasp to bend her abdomen (c) when she wants to sting and to breathe. You can see, as she stands, how it keeps moving up and down all the time. This is because she is breathing. How do you think she does it? Not through her mouth as we do, but through her sides.

If you look closely at the grasshopper you will see along the sides of his body, some little black dots, one in each ring. These are breathing holes, and through them the air goes in and out.

They are smaller in a wasp, but they are there, and she is pumping the air in and out of there.

Now that we have put aside the spider and the centipede, those that remain are true insects. But there is a difference between the daddy-long-legs and the rest, which you must notice. This is that they all have four wings and he has only two. This would be very strange if it were not that we can find some remains of the right number. He has two little knobs (k) behind his front wings, and with these he balances himself. So he has two wings and the stumps of two more.

There is a great deal more to be learnt about these insects. But I want you to remember now that they have six legs; that their body is divided into three parts: that you can see the rings in their hind body or abdomen; that their legs and wings grow on the front body or thorax; and that they never breathe through their mouths. Also that while bees, butterflies, and beetles have four wings, flies have two wings and two stumps.

Find as many insects as you can, and notice their different parts.

LESSON II.

PARTS OF A CATERPILLAR.

IN the last lesson we found the full-grown insects very easily. But it is often more difficult to know some of them when they are young. Grasshoppers, crickets, and plant-lice, when they come out of the egg, are very much the same as when they are grown up, except that they have no wings. But the daddy-long-legs begins its life as a grub underground. The lady-bird when young is a kind of caterpillar and runs over the plants eating plant-lice. And beetles are grubs with six small legs before they grow into perfect beetles with wings.

The caterpillars of Moths and Butterflies are easy to find, so we will look at one in this lesson. There is hardly any time in the summer that you cannot find a caterpillar. Those of the Orange-tipped Butterfly come out first in April. In May the Cabbage Butterfly lays her eggs, and soon the caterpillars are eating the young cabbage leaves. A little later you may find among the nettles the black caterpillars with white spots which will turn in June into the Peacock Butterfly; or the dark

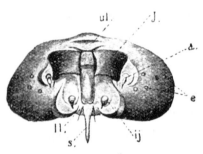

CATERPILLAR'S HEAD.

ul. Upper Lip. *j.* Jaws. *a.* Antennae.
e. Small Eyes. *ij.* Inner Jaws.
ll. Lower Lip. *s.* Spinning Tube.

green caterpillars of the Red Admiral. These are hidden in a bunch of leaves generally tied up with caterpillar silk.

If you do not find either of these you cannot miss the heaps of little black caterpillars striped with yellow which feed under the leaves of nettles, and turn into the small Tortoiseshell Butterfly. These caterpillars are very useful in killing nettles, so the butterfly is one you should always be glad to see. Then towards the autumn the caterpillars of the big Hawk-moths do a great deal of mischief. If you go out in the evening or early morning you may find the caterpillar of the Spurge Hawk-moth feeding on the green spurge in the hedges. It is a fine creature three inches long, with three bright lines on its back, and yellow spots on each ring.

But the most common one, which I have often found, is

the caterpillar of the Privet Hawk-moth, which feeds in the evening on the privet hedge or the lilac bushes. It is from three to four inches long, and is a bright apple-green, with seven sloping violet stripes on its sides, and a horn at the end of its body. Its head is green, edged with black, and the breathing holes on its sides are circled with bright orange.

It destroys the hedges terribly, for it is very hungry and wants to store up food so that it may grow into a moth. Though its body is soft, its head is hard and horny, and as its mouth has nothing to do in breathing, or making any noise, it can be used all the time for eating. It is made of a great many pieces, but the parts you can see well are the large upper lip (*u l*) and the two broad strong outer jaws (*j*) which move to and fro sideways as it gnaws the leaf. As soon as a piece is cut off the caterpillar tucks it into his inner jaws (*i j*), where it is chewed and swallowed. Under the jaws is the flat lower lip (*l l*), through which passes a little tube. Look well at this tube (*s*). It is the place from which comes the silk, which he uses to spin his cocoon, in which he sleeps while his butterfly body is growing.

You remember we read in Book I. that the spider spins her web out of silk which comes from six little pockets under her body. But a caterpillar or a silkworm brings its silk out of its mouth.

Now look at the legs. There are three pairs, one on each ring of the thorax. They have joints in them and claws at the end. These are true legs, and they are hard and horny like the head. When the caterpillar turns into a moth these six legs will remain. But it has also some cushion feet, on the other rings of its body, which it uses to hold fast to the twigs. These are not true legs, but only fleshy cushions with a ring of hooks under them, and they will disappear with the caterpillar's body when the moth grows up. There are generally four pairs of cushion feet behind the true legs, and two pairs at the end of the body, but some caterpillars do not have so many. Do you know those called "Loopers," which bend their body into an arch or loop? You may often find them on the currant bushes, where they do a great deal of mischief. They have only six true legs and four cushion feet at the end of their body, and they walk in a curi-

ous fashion. They hold firmly to the twig by their front legs, and then draw up their cushion feet till their body makes a loop in the air. Then they let go with their front legs and lift up their head like an elephant raises his trunk, and stretch forward further up the twig.

1. CUSHION FEET OF CATERPILLAR.
2. JOINTED LEGS.

As a caterpillar is always eating, his skin becomes so full that there comes a time when he cannot put in any more food. Then he remains quiet for a few hours, and swells out his rings. His skin splits and he creeps out, with a new soft skin ready underneath. This will stretch, and very soon he is eating away as merrily as ever.

He does this about five times in his caterpillar life, and then he stops eating and remains without moving for some days. His colour fades, and when he splits his skin and shuffles it off, all the parts of the butterfly or moth are to be seen underneath, soft and unfinished. Soon a kind of gum oozes out over them. This hardens and keeps the tender body safe from harm while it is growing.

Now he is called a *chrysalis*, or sometimes a *pupa* or doll;

and, indeed, he looks like a crumpled doll as you see his legs bent together and his head folded down over them under the hard gum. The pupa of a butterfly is generally broad at the top and narrow at the bottom, and it has ridges and prickles on it. But the pupas of moths are shaped more like an egg, and are smooth. Moths generally wrap their pupa in a silk bag or cocoon, but butterflies leave theirs naked, and fasten it to a stem or a blade of grass with a silken cord.

The caterpillar of the Hawk-moth works its way down into the ground and lies in a hole which it lines with silk. I had one in a large flower-pot once for many months. After about seven months, or sometimes much longer, the pupa wriggles up to the top of the ground, and then breaks through its cover and comes out as a moth.

Bring in some caterpillars, each with the plant on which you find it. Keep them fed and watch their changes.

LESSON III.
FAMILIAR MOTHS.

WHEN Moths creep out of their cases they no longer do us any harm. They spread their wings and fly about sipping honey from the flowers. Their strong jaws have almost disappeared, and feathery lips take their place. Their inner jaws have grown very long, and are rolled together into a long double tube— very like a tiny elephant's trunk. When the insect is not using this trunk it is rolled up under its lip, but when it wants to reach the honey in the flowers it unrolls the trunk and thrusts it into the blossoms.

In the early morning, or evening in August, you may see the

1. PRIVET HAWK MOTH.   2. CATERPILLAR.   3. CHRYSALIS.
4.TIGER MOTH.   5. CLEARWING MOTH.

Privet Hawk-moth with its beautiful rose-coloured wings striped with black, thrusting its head into the honeysuckle in the hedge. Or the large brown Humming-bird moth may be hovering in the sunshine over a bed of flowers in the garden, or sucking honey out of the deep flowers of the evening primrose. You may know it partly by the humming noise it makes with its wings, and partly because it does not settle on the flowers, but sucks as it flies.

Then there is the Death's-head Hawk-moth, which is the largest moth in England, and has this curious name because the grey marks on the back of its thorax are something like a skull. It has brown front wings, and yellow hind wings, with dark bands across them, and its feelers and trunk are very short. You may find it, if you look out after sunset in the autumn, fluttering over the hedge, for it is not nearly so rare as people think, only it always flies by night.

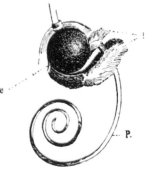

HEAD OF A MOTH.
e. Large Eye. *l*. Lips.
p. Proboscis or Trunk.

If you get one of these big moths you will be surprised to see how different it is from the caterpillar out of which it grows. The six legs are still there on the three rings of the tho-rax, but there are four splendid wings above them. These wings are made of very fine transparent skin, and are covered all over with scales, which are arranged like tiles on a roof. However carefully you take hold of a moth or a butterfly you will always find some fine dust left on your fingers. Each grain of this dust is a lovely scale, and it is these which give the moth its beautiful colours. Moths and butterflies are called Lepi-

doptera, because this word means "scale-winged." The caterpillar had six small eyes, so tiny that we did not notice them.
The moth has these still, but it has besides two glorious globes
on each side of its head, cut into hundreds of little windows,
so that the moth can look every way, although the eyes do not
move. The eyes of the Death's-head moth shine like red lamps
in the dark night.

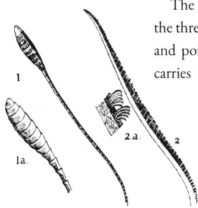

The moth is plainly divided into
the three parts. Its hind body is oval
and pointed, its broad front body
carries its legs and wings, and its
head carries the big eyes (e),
the delicate feelers, and the
sucking trunk. The feelers
or antennæ of moths are
broad in the middle and
pointed at the end, and
they have tiny feathers on
them. By this you may
know moths from butter-

1, 1a. ANTENNAE OF BUTTERFLIES.
2. ANTENNAE OF THE PRIVET
    HAW-MOTH WITH PLUMES AND
    SCALES (2a)

flies. For the antennæ of butterflies are nearly always round
and thick at the ends like a club and have no feathers on them.

Another difference between them is, that butterflies fold
their wings upwards over their backs so that the upper side of
the wings touch each other, while moths lay theirs down on
their backs like a roof on a house.

One common moth you may find is the Goat-moth. It has
a short body and brownish white wings with wavy black lines
on them. You will find it resting on the leaves of the willow or
poplar. It does not fly about much, for it has no trunk, and

does not eat any food during its short moth life. It only wants to find a place on which to lay its eggs, which will hatch into a naked red grub. This grub will bore its way into the tree and live there for years, eating the wood.

Many moth grubs live inside trunks and branches. If you look over the currant bushes on a hot summer's day you will often find a pretty little moth with a narrow yellow and black

SIX-SPOT BURNET MOTH WITH IT'S CATERPILLAR
AND COCOON.

body, thin legs, long feelers and clear transparent wings, very unlike most moths. This is one of the Clearwing-moths, which have scales round the edge of their wings only. It is so lazy that you will easily catch it, and it looks so like a gnat that it is called the Gnat Clearwing. This moth lays its eggs in the twigs of the currant bushes, and its little yellow caterpillar, with a black line on its back, eats its way into the pith of the twigs. You should always clear away the dead or faded twigs on the currant bushes, for fear these caterpillars should be in them.

Another moth which you may find flying in the bright sunshine is of a dark blue-green colour, with six bright crimson spots on its wings. It is the Six-spot Burnet-moth, whose cocoons you may find in May fastened on the blades of long grass in the meadow. By August the moth is out and flits from flower to flower.

There is one more moth which you will like to know, because its caterpillar is the Woolly Bear, or Hairy Man, which curls itself up in a ball when you pick it up. It is very fond of feeding on the lettuces and strawberries, and when it is ready to change it bites off its long hairs and weaves them into its cocoon. When the moth comes out it runs about the flower beds in the evening and does not fly very high. But everyone knows it as the Tiger-moth, for it is the grandest moth we have. Its front wings are cream coloured with wavy brown stripes on them. The hind ones are bright scarlet spotted with black. Its thorax has a bright red band on it, and its abdomen is scarlet with black bars. If you can find a Woolly Bear in the early summer and keep it in a box with a piece of wire over it and give it plenty of dead nettles to eat you may see its cocoon and the grand Tiger-moth which comes out of it.

Try to find a Hawk-moth, a Clearwing-moth, a Tiger-moth, and the cocoon of the Burnet-moth. Bring in caterpillars and cocoons, when you can find them, always with a piece of the plant on which they feed.

LESSON IV.

FAMILIAR BUTTERFLIES.

THERE are not nearly so many butterflies as there are moths. But as the moths often fly at night, we know butterflies best, because they flutter about in the bright sunshine. Their caterpillars do not do so much harm in the garden as the moth caterpillars, except those of the Cabbage butterfly, which we read about in Book III.

You will find it very interesting, in the spring and early summer, to look for the chrysalis of each common butterfly, and keep them in a box with a piece of coarse muslin over it, so as to watch when they come out.

If you do this you will see their colours much better than by catching them, because when they first come out of their sheath, their wings are not battered with wind and rain. And you need not kill them, when you have looked at them you can set them free to enjoy the sunshine.

It is curious that so many butterflies lay their eggs on the leaves of stinging nettles. Perhaps it is because the cows and sheep will not eat these plants, so the eggs are safe. The Peacock butterfly, the small Tortoiseshell, and the Red Admiral all leave their eggs on nettles. It is there that you will find their pupas or chrysalises. Let me tell you how to know them.

The eggs of the Peacock butterfly are gummed in patches under the nettle leaves, and in June you may find the little black caterpillars spotted with white all feeding together in groups. Early in July they will each of them have spun a little cushion of silk under some leaf, by which the curious stiff

BUTTERFLIES.

1. PEACOCK BUTTERFLY ON WING. 1a. AT REST. 2. CATERPILLAR.
3. CHRYSALIS. 4. BRIMSTONE BUTTERFLY. 5. CHRYSALIS.
6. ORANGE-TIP BUTTERFLY. 7. CHRYSALIS. 8. FEMALE AT REST.
9. SMALL HEATH BUTTERFLY. 10. AT REST.

chrysalis hangs head downwards, looking like a brown shining shell.

If you carry home either the caterpillar (2), or the chrysalis, you will find that about the end of July a glorious butterfly (1) will come out. Its hind wings are brown and its front wings bright red and blue, and on each of the four wings there is a large bright eye-spot, like the eyes on a peacock's tail. The body is dark blue, and the feelers on the head are long and thin, with knobs at the end. But when the butterfly shuts its wings (1a), all the bright colours are hidden and the whole insect is brown like the trunk of a tree, with pale edges like wood newly cut, so that the birds are not so likely to see it when it is resting.

But, if you bring home another chrysalis from the nettles by mistake, a different butterfly will surprise you. This one has wings much notched round the edge, and they are coloured black with red markings and white spots. It is the Red Admiral, whose pupa also hangs head downwards under nettle leaves. You will not make this mistake if you find the caterpillar, for it is not black like that of the Peacock butterfly, but dark green with a yellow line on its sides, and it has spikes all over it. It feeds on nettle leaves which it ties round itself with silken threads. And you must remember that these green and yellow caterpillars will turn into Red Admirals.

Again, you may find a bunch of nettle leaves tied together with silk, which have many caterpillars inside them. These will be very spiny, and have four yellow stripes on their black bodies. They will turn into small Tortoiseshell butterflies.

Unless you know these three kinds of caterpillars well, the safe way is to bring them all home and keep them till the butterflies come out, and then notice many little differences which I cannot give you here.

On the thistles you may find another caterpillar which draws the leaves round it, and whose chrysalis has gold spots upon it. This will turn into a reddish brown butterfly called the Painted Lady. In some years there are very few of these, while in other years they are plentiful.

Our next search shall be among the alder trees by the riverside either in the early spring or about the end of July, for there are two broods of this butterfly.

You must look among the small twigs for a pretty green chrysalis with red dots on it, something like a ribbed shell. It will be tied round the middle to the stem of the twig by a fine rope of silk. Notice how cleverly the caterpillar has swung it, so that the heavy broad end

1. TORTOISESHELL BUTTERFLY.
2. AT REST.
3. CHRYSALIS.

balances the long thin one. Then cut off the twig and take it home. The chrysalis will turn into the Brimstone butterfly (4), whose pale yellow wings have four red spots on them. You will know it quite well, for it is generally the first butterfly to come out in the spring.

Next we shall have to look low down among the plants by the roadside. There are some with white and pink flowers whose petals are in the form of a cross. They are called rock-cress and bittercress, and if you can find out which they are, and look under their leaves you may find a most curious chrysalis shaped like a boat pointed at both ends. This will turn into the Orange-tip butterfly (6), which has a broad orange patch on the tip of its front wings. This butterfly is very gay when it is flying, but when it settles (8) and folds its wings upwards, it can scarcely be seen on the flowers of the wild parsley from which it sips honey. This is because the underside of the wings are dotted with green and like the tiny parsley flowers with their white petals and green centres.

Another common butterfly is the small Heath (9) which may be seen any fine day in June or September sipping honey from the heath on the common. It feeds as a green caterpillar on the tall grasses, and comes out a pretty little butterfly with tawny yellow wings, with a round eye-spot.

Now you know how to look for caterpillars, and chrysalises, and butterflies, you can learn about them for yourself. Anywhere on the violet beds you may find the spiny caterpillars of the pretty striped and dotted butterflies called Fritillaries. Blue butterflies are found mostly in chalk districts, though the Common Blue lives almost everywhere, and you may often see the little Copper butterflies flying with it, their dark glittering wings gleaming amongst the lovely blues. And wherever you see a butterfly on the wing you should try to follow it till it alights, for one of the most interesting points to notice, among all butterflies, is how the under colour of their wings helps to hide them when they are resting, while the upper colour is bright and gay.

Bring in caterpillars and chrysalises, and watch them. Notice the plant on which the caterpillar feeds. Compare the under surface of their wings with the plants on which they settle.

LESSON V.
INJURIOUS BEETLES.

ALL living creatures must hunt for food, and insects eat a great deal for their size. Beetles are very heavy feeders. They eat most when they are grubs, but some, like Cockchafers and Tiger-beetles, eat almost as much when they are full-grown and have their wings.

There are plant-eating beetles, and beetles which feed on other insects and animals. Altogether there are more than 3,000 species of beetles in the British Isles. It is useful to know what kind of food a beetle eats, for some do good work in the fields and gardens, while others do great injury to the crops.

One of the most mischievous is the Cockchafer. You know him quite well when he flies in your face in the evening. But perhaps you do not know him as a grub, when he lives for three or four years underground, and eats the roots of the grass, corn, and vegetables. If you see plants in the cornfield or garden looking sickly and yellow, and drooping their leaves although the ground is damp, it is most likely that there is a grub underneath, and it may be the grub of a Cockchafer.

Dig up the plant and you will find an ugly white creature

like a huge maggot, almost as thick as your little finger, with a red head and very strong jaws. It has six long legs, with five joints, growing on the rings behind its head, and is so full of food that it can hardly crawl. The end of its tail is swollen into a thick cushion, and you can see the breathing all along its sides very clearly because it is so distended with food. You remember that it does not take in breath through its mouth, so it can go on eating all the time. If you had not disturbed it, it would have crept on from plant to plant across the field, doing nothing but eat for three years. It goes down deeper in the ground in winter to keep warm during the frosty weather.

At last in the autumn of the third year it draws itself together, and leaves off eating for nearly eight months. If you can find one at this time you will be able to see the parts of the real beetle crumpled up under the clear skin, and for the last few months it will be a full-grown sleeping cockchafer.

Then, when the warm summer comes, it crawls up above ground and flies into the trees, eating their leaves as greedily as it ate their roots while it was a grub. This is the time to catch and kill them, for they only live about a month, and meanwhile the mother cockchafer lays the eggs which will hatch into grubs.

You will be surprised to see how different the beetle is from the white grub you found underground. It is now a flying insect, about half an inch long, with brown powdery wing-cases, covering a pair of transparent wings. Its hind-body, or abdomen, ends in a fine point, and on its head it carries a pair of feelers tipped with broad folds like a half-open fan.

These folds are very handsome in the male Chafer, but much smaller in the female (2), and by this you may know the

DESTRUCTIVE BEETLES.
1. Male Cockchafer.   2. Female.   3. Grub.
4. Pupa.   5. Cock-Beetle or Skipjack.

mother which will lay the eggs. You must catch and kill these last if you want to save your crops, and the most merciful way to do this is to drop them into boiling water. A crushed beetle is a long time dying, but boiling water kills them at once.

You will find that they rest in the daytime on favourite trees, and, if you spread a cloth underneath, you may beat the boughs and so catch a good many. Farmers use gas-lime and other dressings to kill the grubs in the ground.

Another very mischievous creature is the young of the Skip-jack or Click-beetle. All children know these little beetles, though perhaps you may not know their name. They are narrow and flat, about half an inch long, with very short legs. The most common one in England has reddish wing-cases, striped with long furrows, and a black head and thorax. Boys love to pick them up, and turn them on their backs, for they bend themselves up in the middle so as to rest on their head and tail. Then with a sudden jerk and a click they straighten themselves, so that their back hits your hand and sends them up in the air, and they come down the right way up. Sometimes they fall again on their backs, then they rest a little and begin again.

These amusing little creatures are very destructive when they are grubs, for the wireworms we know so well are the young of the Click-beetle. If you find a wireworm and look at it carefully you will see that it is not a worm, but has the six legs on the rings behind its head, by which you know that it is an insect. Wireworms feed on the roots of most plants. They are long and narrow like a piece of wire, and are generally of a reddish yellow colour, and have very tough skins.

The Click-beetle lays her eggs in meadows, and among the roots of plants, and the wireworm when it is hatched often

feeds for five years before turning into a beetle. Therefore
Click-beetles must be destroyed, and salt and lime sprinkled on
the earth to kill the grubs.

Unfortunately the pretty little Weevil-beetles are also very
destructive. We read in Book I. about the Nut-weevil, and almost every plant and tree has some weevil which attacks it.
There is the weevil of the apple-blossom (4), the Pea-weevil (1
and 2), the Bean-weevil (3), the Furze-weevil, the Vine-weevil,
and many others. They all begin life as little soft maggots with
no true legs, but only cushion feet, and with horny heads and
sharp jaws.

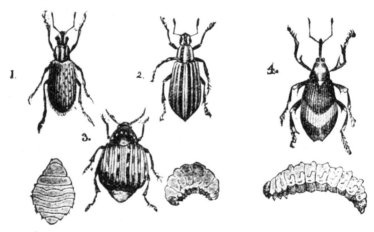

1. SPOTTED PEA-WEEVIL.   2. STRIPED PEA-WEEVIL.
3. BEAN WEEVIL.   4. APPLE-BLOSSOM WEEVIL

You may know the full-grown weevils by their prominent
snouts, sometimes broad and sometimes long. They are beautiful little creatures with polished wings which shine like jew-
els, and bright eyes; but as grubs they destroy the flowers,
fruits, and green shoots everywhere.

Some of the most curious are the Stem-boring weevils.
They have long snouts and very sharp jaws, and their feet have

hairy pads underneath with sharp hooks at the end, so that they can cling firmly to smooth stems. If you search on the poplar tree in summer you may find a lovely Stem-borer with shining green wings and red eyes; and on the fruit trees of the orchard you are almost sure to find the Steel-blue weevil which lays her eggs in their shoots.

When the mother stem-borer wants to lay, she bores a hole in a young shoot with her snout and forces an egg into it. When she has laid several in this way, she sets to work to cut off the shoot with her sharp jaws. This often takes her some weeks, and if you see the hanging shoot and burn it you will destroy the grubs. But at last, when it hangs by only a thread of bark, she weighs it down, and it falls to the ground, where the grub feeds in peace when it is hatched.

Try to find Cockchafers—male, female, and grub. Bring in a Click-beetle and a Wireworm. Find as many weevils as you can; and twigs, flowers, and fruit with grubs in them.

LESSON VI.
USEFUL BEETLES.

WE cannot help destroying some beetles when there are so many that they eat our crops. But it is pleasant to know that there are others which do us so much good that we need not wage war upon them.

The Tiger-beetles, for example, are very hungry creatures; but, as they feed on other insects, they destroy the weevil and cockchafer grubs, wireworms and caterpillars, and so save our plants. Their name is given to them because they are so fierce and cunning. They are not very large—our common tiger-beetle is not more than three-quarters of an inch in length—but their long slender legs are very strong, and they can fly very fast.

There are always plenty running about in the hot sun across dry, dusty fields or commons in summer. Their wing-cases are a beautiful shining green colour shot with copper, and dotted with five yellow spots. They run very gracefully, and so fast that you will find it difficult to catch one. Just as you think you have it, it will suddenly open its wing-cases, spread its delicate transparent wings, and be off almost before you can see it go.

But if you can catch it, you will see that it has large eyes standing out on each side of its head and two sharp jagged jaws for tearing its prey, while the lower ones are covered with stiff bristles which help to hold it.

And now you must look for its grub, which is a very curious creature. The best way to find it is to go to some soft part of a sandy field where you have seen the Tiger-beetles running about. Then look at any small holes in the sand, and try to find one which leads to a tunnel in the ground. The grub of the Tiger-beetle sits at the mouth of this tunnel to catch insects as they pass. It will disappear as soon as you come near, but if you put a blade of grass into the hole and shake it, the grub will grasp the blade, and you can pull it out.

Then you can see the tools it uses. It is a long soft white grub with a horny head, and jaws like sickles, and, besides its six brown spiny feet, it has two soft humps on its back with little hooks on them. As soon as this grub is hatched in the ground, it scoops a tunnel in the soft sand with its spiny legs, and pulls itself up to the top, holding on by its legs and the hooks on its back. Its head just fills the hole, and as it is a poor weakly creature and cannot move fast, it keeps quiet till some

USEFUL BEETLES.

1. Tiger Beetle. 2. Cocktail Beetle. 3. Sexton Beetle burying a Mouse.

insect passes, and then darts its head out and pulls its victim down. If you have the patience to find some of these tunnels, and sit still and watch, you may see the grub catch its prey.

The Rove or Cocktail-beetles, which we found in the first lesson, are very useful in eating insects, though they are not beautiful. But the Ground-beetles, which have only small wings under their wing cases, and seldom fly, are the best hunters. You may sometimes see a good-sized beetle with long legs running along through the grass. Its body is very dark, shaded with red and violet. This is the Violet Ground-beetle, and it is hunting for grubs and wireworms.

There are some very curious beetles not difficult to find which will interest you. These are the Sexton, or Burying-beetles. When you see a dead mouse or bird lying in some part of the field or garden, pick it up quietly. If it has been there a few days it will already have a bad smell, and you are almost sure to find underneath it two or more beetles with thick bodies and strong legs. They are generally black with red feelers, and two light red bands on their abdomen. These are Sexton-beetles, which have scented the dead body and flown, often for some distance, to bury it.

They scrape away the soft ground underneath, till the body sinks down, and then they drag the earth over it. Why do you think they do this? Because the mother beetle wants to lay her eggs there that the grubs may feed on the flesh. She does this as soon as the animal is buried, and in a few days the grubs are hatched. They are narrow, and each has six legs and a number of spines along its back. With these it wriggles through the flesh, and eats away till it buries itself in the ground and turns into a beetle.

A great many beetles are useful to us by eating dead and living animals. Among these are the little black shining Mimic-beetles, which draw up their legs and pretend to be dead when they are touched, and the Glow-worms, which shine so brightly in the lanes in the summer nights.

A good gardener who sees a glow-worm in a hedge will always pick it up gently, and put it in his garden when he has the chance. For the young of the glow-worm is a soft grub, which works its way into the shells of small snails and feeds upon them.

If you find a dry snail-shell with a white grub in it, it will most likely be the grub of the glow-worm. You may know it by a tuft of white threads on its tail, which it uses to brush off the slime of the snail from its back.

When they are full-grown you will find the mother glow-worm (1) very easily at night, because she gives out such a bright light. She has no wings, and you might take her for a slug if you did not notice her six little legs. The male glow-worm (2) has two spots of light near his tail. But he is not so bright as the female. He has long soft wing-cases and broad wings, with which he often flies into a lighted room when the window is left open.

The last useful beetle we can mention is the little Ladybird. She feeds all her life long on the plant bugs and aphides which destroy our plants. Wherever there are plant-lice, there the ladybird lays a bunch of yellow eggs and, when they are hatched, the long dark grubs clamber up the plant stalks and poke the lice into their mouths with their front feet. After a time each one glues its tail to a leaf and hangs till it becomes a ladybird,

GLOW WORMS.
1. Female with glowing light.　2. Male with faint light.　3. Grub.

and then it flies away to feed on plant-lice on some other bush and to lay more eggs.

Bring in a Tiger-beetle, and try to find its grub. Search for Sexton-beetles under dead animals. Bring in a Mimic-beetle. Find a male and female glow-worm. Look for the grub of the Ladybird.

LESSON VII.

WASPS AND THEIR WAYS.

WE all like Butterflies because they are pretty, and Bees because they give us honey. But no one likes Wasps, for we are always afraid that they will sting, and they spoil our garden fruit. Yet wasps are very industrious and interesting. They act as scavengers, eating offal, raw meat, and insects, and they never sting unless they are frightened. You may be stung by pressing a wasp without knowing it. But people are very silly who flap them, and keep dodging about when they are near, for if you sit quite still they will not hurt you.

We are obliged to kill wasps, or we should be overrun by them and have no fruit, and the best way is to keep a good look out in the spring and early summer. The few big ones which come out then are queen wasps, or mothers, and each one will found a nest. It is more merciful to kill these, than to have to take nests in the summer, when there may be as many as 3,000 or 4,000 in each. Most boys have seen a wasps' nest dug out at night, but perhaps you have never looked at one carefully. Let us see how it is made.

When the queen-wasp comes out from under the moss or grass, where she has spent the winter, she looks out for a hole in the ground, left perhaps by a mouse or a mole. Creeping into it, she makes it larger by biting the earth and kicking it out with her hind feet. Then she flies away and scrapes small pieces of fibre off the trees and plants. You may sometimes see her scraping window frames or posts with her jaws. She is getting shreds of wood. With these she goes back to the hole, and works them up, with some gluey matter from her mouth, into a kind of greyish paper or cardboard.

Before it hardens she plasters this into the top of the hole, making a thick lump, which she glues to the roots of plants. Then she starts afresh for more fibre, and with it builds a few cells under the lump.

She lays an egg in each, and then goes on making more paper and more cells. In about eight days the first eggs are hatched into legless grubs, and she feeds them with honey and insects, still going on with her work. In about three weeks the grubs spin their cocoons, and in another week they come out as working wasps. After that, some come out almost every day, and the queen-wasp leaves them to do the work of building the nest and feeding the grubs, while she only lays eggs.

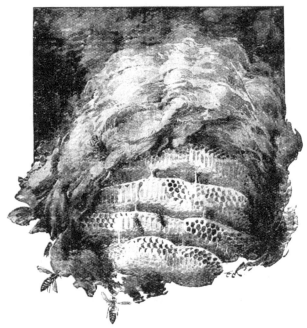

INSIDE OF COMMON WASPS' NEST.

They not only build cells, they also cover the nest with a papery dome of several layers, which hangs like an open umbrella, from the lump at the top. When they have finished one comb it is like a round plate, and is smooth above, with a great number of cells underneath, all opening downwards.

The wasps then make several gluey pillars under this comb to hold up a new one below which they form in the same way as the first. So they go on till August, when there may be fifteen or sixteen flat round plates one below the other, joined by a number of pillars. Then they draw the papery dome in at the bottom so that the whole nest is a round or oval-shaped ball. As wasps do not store honey, these combs are only cells for grubs. The papery covering prevents the wet soaking in from the bank.

In August they build larger cells, out of which come males or drones which have longer antenna; than the workers and queen-wasps. These queens are larger than either the males or workers. They soon fly out of the nest and pair with the drones

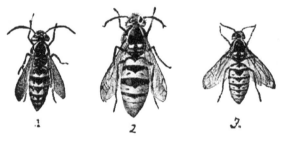

I. MALE.   2. QUEEN WASP.   3. WORKER.

and as winter comes on the wasps kill any grubs which remain, and, growing sleepy and dull, die themselves, leaving only the queen-wasps to sleep till next spring. Then if you know where there is an old nest you can dig it carefully out and see the long tunnel in the bank, along which the wasps went in, so that no one might know where their nest was.

Some wasps build under the roofs of houses, especially the large wasps called Hornets, unless they choose the old trunk of a tree. If you look in a wood you may sometimes find the nest of the Wood-wasp hanging under the bough of a tree, though you would scarcely notice it unless you follow a Wood-wasp home. They are built like the other nests, only they have a thick papery column down the middle.

Besides the common wasps there are a great many smaller kinds, some of which you may find. They are very interesting, because they carry insects into a hole and bury them with their eggs, so that the young grub may have food when it is hatched.

There is a pretty little wasp, generally called the Wall-wasp, which you may see in June or July biting the mortar in the garden wall or making holes in a sandy bank. It is smaller and blacker than the common wasp, and has a few bright yellow bands on its hind body. It scoops out a tunnel in the mortar and leaves the pieces sticking round the hole. Then after going in to see that all is right it comes out and flies away, coming back presently with a small green caterpillar. It carries this in and goes off for another, and so it goes on till it has brought about fifteen or twenty.

If you dig out the mortar along the wall, so as to open this tunnel, you will find at the end an egg hanging by a thread. The wasp put the egg there before she went for the first caterpillar. Between this egg and the hole the fifteen little caterpillars will be lying curled up one beyond the other. The curious thing is that they are not dead. The wasp has only stupefied them with her stings so that they do not try to escape. If you do not break into the nest she will stop the hole up with the pieces of mortar round the edge and leave it. Then when the grub has eaten the caterpillars and turned into a wasp it will bite its way out.

Then you may find some of the Sand-wasps, which dig so many holes in the sandbanks on heaths, or in the lanes and gardens, wherever it is sunny and warm. One of these, called the

SOLITARY WASPS.

1. Wall Wasp.   2. Sand Wasp.

Hairy Sand-wasp, puts Spiders in her hole for the grub to eat. She is orange coloured, with a black head and straggling legs. But she is very strong and can drag a big spider to her den.

I have not room to tell you more of these curious wasps, some of which fill their nests with beetles, others with crickets. But now you know about them you will follow any you see and watch their habits for yourself, which is much the best way.

Find an old wasps' nest and try to make a drawing of it. Notice the shape of the common wasp and compare it with any others you find. Notice particularly the difference in the thread joining the abdomen to the thorax.

LESSON VIII.

SOLITARY BEES.

WE all know the Hive-bee well, but perhaps you have not noticed that there are other kinds of bees flying in the garden. Some of these are about the same size as the hive-bee; some are much smaller, and they are differently marked.

Most of these are solitary bees. There are no neuters among them, only males and females living in pairs. Others live in great numbers in the holes of sandy banks, but do not work together.

If you have ivy growing on your cottage, you must often have noticed small bees flitting in and out of the flower. Among these there will most likely be one, about half an inch long, with a black body covered with a tawny down. She will have two little horns on her head, and is called the "Two-horned Osmia".

If you can watch one and follow her, you may see her fly into some old rotten post, or tree-stump. Then if you cut into the post near the hole you will find a curious nest. For this bee bores a long tunnel and builds a waxen cell at the bottom. Here she lays an egg and puts round it bee-bread, made of pollen and honey from the flowers. She has no groove in her leg like the hive-bee, so she carries the sticky pollen in the thick hairs under her body, and scrapes it off with a comb on her feet.

When she has laid the egg and put in food, she seals the cell with wax, and begins another on the top of it. So she goes on till she has filled the tunnel.

But how is the bottom bee to get out? Her egg was laid first and she has eight or ten others on the top of her. Strange to say they wait for each other. They all become perfect bees about the same time, and, if one below is ready sooner than the others, she eats through the cover of her cell and tries to push past her neighbour. But if the one above is so big that the bee cannot get by without hurting her, she waits patiently till all are ready.

Another little bee which you may often find is the Sleeper bee, so-called because she often sleeps in the blossoms of flowers, where you may find her. She is thin and black with a square head and strong jaws, and she has a little yellow down on her hind body or abdomen. She too burrows in posts, but very often she makes her nest inside a large straw. In olden days, when cottages were thatched, hundreds of these bees would build in the larger straws of the thatch, and might be heard buzzing about the roof.

Then there is another bee which you cannot help finding.

SOLITARY BEES.

1. Osmia Bees. 2. Sleeper Bee.
3. Leaf-Cutting Bee. 4. Carder Bee.

This is the Leaf-cutting bee. Have you not seen the leaves of rose-trees with pieces like a half-moon cut out of their edge? If you watch you may see a bee doing this work.

She is about the same size as a hive-bee, but rather stouter, and her body is black with soft brown hairs over it. She clings to the leaf and turns round in a circle biting as she goes. Just before she has finished she opens her wings and so balances herself in the air. Then, when the last bite is made, she flies off with the piece of leaf carried between her feet and her jaws.

She goes to a hole in the ground, which is straight down for a little way, and then turns, and runs along under the surface. Here she packs the leaf in and goes back for more. With several pieces she makes a

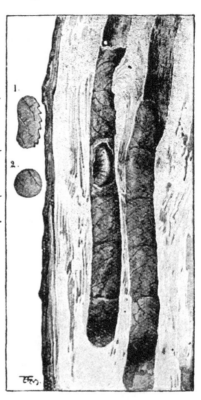

NEST OF LEAF-CUTTING BEE
IN A TREE.

One Cell cut open showing the Grub.
1. Leaf cut for the Sides.
2. Leaf cut for Bottom of each
Thimble.

little thimble, in which she lays an egg, with food round it, and closes it with three or four round pieces. Then she begins another thimble, pushing it in, so that it fits a little way into the last one. In this way she builds about seven cells, each with its egg and bee-bread, for the grubs to feed on till they turn into bees. Though you will easily see the bees cutting the leaves, you will not so easily find their tunnels, for they fill in the earth again at the top, so that the entrance cannot be seen. The best way is to follow a bee which has been cutting a leaf, but she is so quick you will have to be quick too. Sometimes she makes

her hole in a willow tree when the wood is soft.

There is another Osmia which makes its nest in the stem of the bramble. It hollows out the pith and covers the cells with it. When you see a blackberry stalk with the end bitten off, you may as well cut down a little way with your knife and see if there is a tunnel in it, with bee-cells, or wasp-cells, inside.

Another very curious bee, called the Carder bee, lines its tunnel with fluffy hairs and cotton stripped off plants. You will remem-

NEST OF THE BRAMBLE OSMIA, WITH A YOUNG OSMIA SHOWN IN A CELL.

ber that the ragged robin and wild campion have their stems covered with thick down. The "Carder bees" strip this fluff off the plants, roll it up in a ball, and fly away with it to their nests in the ground, where they use it to make their cells.

Solitary bees do not store honey for the winter like the hive bees. They die off in the autumn, all except some mothers, which creep into holes and sleep till the spring, when they make their nests and lay their eggs.

There are so many of them that I cannot tell you about them all. You must watch for yourselves, and you will soon learn to notice the little holes in the trees and the ground, and in some of them you are sure to find curious creatures.

Notice different kinds of solitary bees, and try to find their tunnels in the spring.

LESSON IX.
HIVE BEES.

HIVE bees are so much at home in our gardens, that I am afraid most people think they know all about them, and take very little notice of them. This is unfortunate, because bee-keeping is very interesting, and many more cottagers might make money by bees, and at the same time become really fond of these busy little insects.

When all the bees in the hive had to be killed each time the honeycombs were taken, we could not get fond of our bees. But now, even cottagers can have boxes and glasses on the top of their hives so as to take the combs without destroying the little friends who fill them for us.

The hive-bee is a wonderful insect. She has three pairs of legs, and two pairs of wings just like a Wasp. But the hind pair of legs is longer than the others, and she has a groove in each of them which makes a kind of basket, into which she packs pollen from the flowers, and carries it home to make bee-bread for her grubs. You may often see a bee going into a hive with both its hind legs heavily laden with sticky pollen. It is puzzling at first to guess how she gets it into the basket, but, if you look lower down her leg, you will see that it is covered with hairs which form a small brush. When she comes out of a flower her hairy body is covered with pollen-dust, and she brushes it off with one leg, making it into a little lump, which she packs into the basket of the other leg.

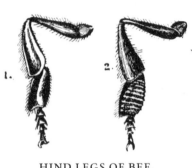

HIND LEGS OF BEE.
1. Outer Side.
2. Inner Side with groove for Honey.

Her mouth is a most useful tool for getting honey. When she is not sucking, her trunk is drawn in under her strong jaws. But when she is feeling for honey, this trunk, which is really a long under lip with a hairy tongue inside it, is thrust into the flower and brings back the honey, which she passes down her throat into a honey-bag, or first stomach.

Then she flies back to the hive. There other bees take the pollen out of her basket as she goes in, and she passes on to the cells, and pours into them the honey from her throat. Some of this honey is used to feed the young bee-grubs, and the rest to fill the honey-combs for the winter.

Sometimes, however, the bee does not pour out the honey, but goes to the top of the hive, and hangs quietly by her front feet. After about four and twenty hours the honey is digested in her stomach, and part of it forms bees-wax, which oozes out under her body into eight little pockets. Then she goes down into the hive, and licks this wax out with her strong jaws, moistens it with her tongue into a kind of paste, and uses it to build the cells of the comb.

It is when the bees are out getting honey and pollen that they are so useful to the gardener. You will remember that the vegetable marrows cannot grow unless the bees carry pollen from one flower to another. Our plants have better flowers and our fruit trees bear better fruit because the bees fly to and fro and carry pollen from one to another.

But if the bee carried it haphazard from one kind of flower to another it would be of very little use, for strange pollen would not make the seeds grow. Watch a bee and you will

BEE HAGING AND SHOWING THE WAX-POCKETS UNDER HER BODY.

find that she very seldom visits more than one kind of flower on the same journey. She will fly from one bed of violets to another, or from apple-tree to apple-tree. But she will not in one journey go from an apple-tree to a pear-tree, nor from a violet to a primrose. We do not know why she does this, but it is very useful to us, and all gardeners should encourage bees in their garden.

And now, if you want to keep bees, you must learn a few simple things. You must always be very gentle and quiet with them. They will soon learn to know you, and to understand that you are not afraid of them.

If you have a straw hive it should measure about sixteen to eighteen inches across, be about eight or nine inches high, and flat on the top, with a hole in it in which a plug is fixed. Put this hive in a warm sheltered part of the garden on a wooden bench about fifteen inches from the ground. Then in May buy a swarm of bees which has just come out from a neighbour's hive. Smear your own hive inside with balm and sugar, and hold it under the bough on which the swarm hangs. Shake the

BEE-HIVE WITH WOODEN SECTIONS ON THE TOP AND GLASS WINDOWS IN THE SIDE.

bough gently till the bees fall in. Turn the hive down on to a piece of wood, and in the evening carry it gently to your garden. The next morning the bees will be busily at work. The big heavy drones will wander about idly, but the smaller working bees will go out and collect honey, hang up in the hive till they have wax in their pockets, and begin to build the comb. If your swarm was the first to leave the hive, the old queen bee, which was in the middle, will soon begin to lay eggs in the cells—about 200 a day. But a second swarm is led by a young queen, and she will fly out with the drones before she settles down in the hive. Now the working bees will be very busy. In two or three days the first eggs are hatched, and the nursing bees feed the grubs with honey and pollen which the other bees bring in. In about five or six days they seal up the mouth of each cell, and the bee-grub spins its silken cocoon, in which it turns into a bee in ten days more. Then it comes out and works with the rest.

The empty cell will soon be filled with honey; but it will be brown, not white and clean like the "virgin" honey which is put into new cells. After about six weeks the queen lays some eggs in larger cells, out of which come males or drones. Then about every three days she lays an egg in a cell like a thimble, on the edge of the comb. The grub in this is fed with special food, and becomes a queen-bee.

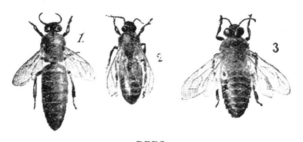

BEES.
1. Queen.   2. Worker.   3. Drone.

Unless you have a hive with a glass window in it you cannot see all this going on. But about the beginning of June you may expect that the hive is getting full of combs and bees. Then is the time to take out the plug at the top, and put on a bell-glass, or a box of wooden sections. In these the bees will make comb which you can take away. You must put in a small piece of comb to tempt the bees to build, and then you must put a straw cover or some old cloths over the whole to keep it warm and dry and dark.

In about a month you will find this upper hive full of honey-comb sealed up in the cells. You can take it off with a cloth dipped in weak Condy's Fluid, for the bees do not like this, and they will not come near you. These sections of honey-comb will be pure and clear, and you can take them away without killing a single bee.

In July you may get one or more new swarms, and then when September comes you must take off the top and cork up the hive for the winter. But remember that you have taken a great part of the bees' store of food and you must feed them with honey and sugar during the cold weather.

Examine three bees—male, female and neuter. Examine trunk and hind legs of the working bee. Get a piece of brown honey-comb with remains of bee-bread and young bees. Compare it with pure honey-comb. Watch a bee among the flowers. Find honey-comb with thimble cells on the edge.

LESSON X.
THE TWO-WINGED FLIES.

THERE are a number of small flying insects which belong to the same family as the Bees and Wasps, such as the Saw-flies, which destroy our vegetables, and the Gall-flies which make those curious galls we found on the oak-tree and other trees. But though we call these "flies" you may always know them from true flies because they have four wings, while all real flies have only two.

Try to collect as many two-winged flies as you can. There will be the common House-fly, the Blue-bottle or Blow-fly, Gnats, Midges, Daddy-long-legs, Horse-flies, and many others.

The House-fly and the Blue-bottle are both very useful in their right place, for they eat decaying matter and dead animals. But they do great harm if we allow them to multiply in the wrong place.

If you have a great number of flies in your house you may be sure that there is dirt somewhere, for the House-fly lays her eggs in dung heaps, dust-heaps, or on any dirt she can find behind a shutter or door, or in an unswept corner.

She lays about 150 at a time, and in a day or two the little legless grubs are hatched, and feed on the dirt. In four or five days they leave off eating and rest in their grub-skin, which grows hard and brown. Then in sum-mer they come out as full-grown flies in about a week. But in winter the hard pupa often lies for months, and people who do not clean their house thoroughly in autumn are likely to have a plague of flies next year.

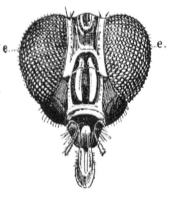

e. ... ... e.

HEAD OF BLOW-FLY
SHOWING THE LARGE
COMPOUND EYES.

The Blue-bottle or Blow-fly lays her eggs *(a)* on meat of any kind, or on the bodies of decaying animals. When her grubs are hatched they are very useful in ridding us of bad-smelling creatures, for they give out a kind of liquid which makes the flesh decay more quickly so that they may eat it.

All boys know "gentils" *(b)* used for fishing. These are the maggots of the Blue-bottle, and when they have done feeding they grow soft inside and draw themselves up into an egg-shape. Then they give out a liquid which hardens their skin

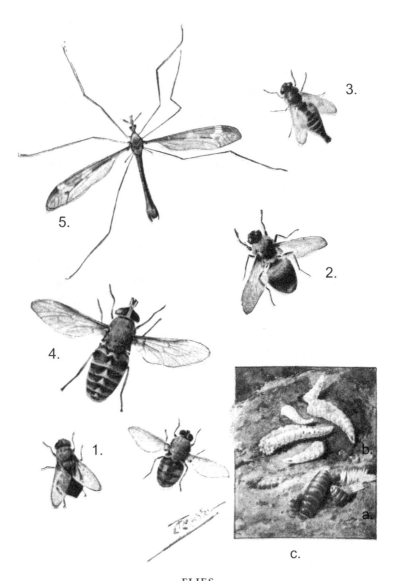

FLIES.
1. Blow-Flies.   2. Oxbot Or Warble Fly.   *a*. Eggs.
b. Maggot. *c*. Pupa.   3. Horse Bot-Fly.   4. Gad-Fly.
5. Daddy-Long-Legs.

into a shiny reddish brown case *(c)*. Inside this the Blue-bottle forms, and then pushes its head out between two little lids at the top of the cocoon.

If you catch a Blue-bottle and put it under a bell-glass with a few grains of sugar you may watch it put out its trunk and feed. You will see that it turns and twists the sugar as if it were playing with it. But all the time it is wetting it with some liquid which it sends down its trunk so as to work the hard lump into syrup which it can suck up. If you press the thorax of a Blue-bottle very gently with your finger and thumb it will put out its trunk and you can see the thick lips at the end with the sucker (A) between them. But you will want a magnifying glass or a microscope to see a little lancet (l) which it has inside its trunk, and which it uses to pierce the skins of fruits, when it wants to suck their juice.

There are two kinds of flies which are much more hurtful than the common fly or the blue-bottle. These are the Gad-flies and the Bot-flies. You know one of the small Gad-flies quite well, for it drops on our hands, or our neck, when we are sitting out of doors, and lets us know that it is there, by giving a sharp bite to suck our blood. We call it the Horse-fly because it teases the horses so much in summer; but there are many others we do not know so well. The largest English Gad-fly is about an inch long.

The Bot-flies are more dangerous than the Gad-flies, for instead of biting with their mouths they prick with a sharp tube

TRUNK OF BLOW
-FLY WITH
THICK LIPS.
A. Sucker.
l. Lancet.

at the end of their abdomen, so as to lay their eggs under the skin of an animal. The Bot-fly or Warble-fly of the ox looks very like a humble bee, only she has two wings instead of four. She has a pointed tube at the end of her body, with which she pricks the skin of the ox, and lays her eggs underneath it. In a short time the eggs hatch, and the maggot irritates the flesh so much that large lumps are seen on the side or back of the animal. If the farmer does not press out the maggots from these lumps, and put a proper dressing on them, the beef of the ox will be poor and bad, and no feeding will make it any better. When the maggot is full-grown it drops to the ground to make its change.

The horse Bot-fly does not put her eggs under the skin, but sticks them, with a little slime from her mouth, to the hairs of the horse on his shoulder or under the knee.

When the egg is ready to break, the warmth of the horse's tongue, as he licks himself, makes it crack and the grub slips down the horse's throat to his stomach. There it feeds, and when it is full-grown passes out with the dung.

The way to check this grub is to keep the skin of the horse clean and the hair short. This Bot-fly is rather larger than the House-fly, with bright yellow markings and a very hairy body.

I wonder how many grubs you know of those gnat-like flies, with thin feelers and legs, which fly in the fields and over the rivers. We read about the gnat in Book II., but you should know the midges, which attack wheat and other grain.

The Wheat-midge is a little orange yellow fly, about the size of a very small gnat. Early on a June morning, when the wheat is in flower, you may shake these midges off the stalks and see them flying near the ground. The mothers have a sharp tube as thin as a hair, with which they lay their eggs in the wheat blossom. There they hatch into little red maggots, which feed on the grain and often destroy half a crop.

You ought to know, too, the grubs of the Daddy-long-legs, which do so much harm to our crops. If you see a Daddy-long-legs clinging to a blade of grass she is most likely thrusting her egg-tube into the ground to lay her eggs.

These hatch into legless brown grubs with strong jaws and a pair of short horns. Farmers call them "Leather Jackets," and you may find them when you are ploughing damp fields. Or you may find the hard pupa, which is shaped like a Daddy-long-legs with its wings folded, its legs drawn up, and two horns on its head. It has spines on its abdomen, with which it will drag itself up when the fly wants to come out.

The best way to get rid of these hurtful grubs is to plough the ground deeply and bury the eggs or maggots, so that they die, or cannot get to the surface, or to put a dressing of gas-lime or other insect-killer on the land. Starlings are very useful in pulling them out of the ground and eating them.

Find grub and pupa of Blue-bottle. Examine a Blue-bottle—legs, body, and proboscis. Try to find House-fly eggs. Bring in a Horse-fly. Try to find the Bot-flies of the ox and the horse. Find a Wheat-midge and its grub; also the grub and pupa of the Daddy-long-legs.

LESSON XI.

CRICKETS AND GRASSHOPPERS.

ALL the insects about which we have been reading are different when they are young from what they are when full grown. But young Crickets and Grasshoppers when they come out of the egg are much the same as when they are older, except that they are smaller and have no wings. They jump and eat and behave in the same way as their parents, and change their coats four or five times. After the last change you can see their wing-cases under the skin, and, when this bursts, they spread their wings and fly.

If you make a cage of wire gauze and put some young crickets in it, and feed them with damp leaves, you may see these changes. But do not try with a muslin cover, as a friend of mine did. For crickets have strong jaws and soon eat their way through.

The little green Grasshoppers of the fields are easy to find, but the large green Grasshopper, is not so common. Still if you know where to look, in the nut-hedges and woods, you may often catch one, and it is a fine insect to examine. His head is well separated from his front body or thorax, and he has two very long feelers which lie back over his body. His jaws are very strong, and if you give him a leaf to eat, under a glass, you can see how they move sideways to cut the food, and the upper and lower lips, through which he passes it to his chewing jaws inside.

If you have caught a female, she will have a curious long tube or egg-layer at the end of her body, which she forces into the ground, to lay her eggs, and this will show you the way that other smaller insects do it.

And now you will want to know how a grasshopper chirps, for you will remember that no insect can make any noise with its mouth. Put your finger gently along, under the left front wing of the great green Grasshopper, close to where it is joined to the body. You will feel that it is rough like a file. The grasshopper rubs this file against the edge of the other wing, and makes the rasping noise.

The small green Grasshopper, which has short feelers standing forward from his head, makes his chirping noise in another way. He has a file on the inside of his hind leg, which he rubs against the top of his wing. This little grasshopper is really a small locust, like those which fly in swarms over Europe, eating every green thing. which comes in their way. Fortunately for us, though he eats very greedily, our little friend is not so destructive as they are. Locusts have no egg laying tube; they drop their eggs into the loose earth and cover them up.

Crickets are very like grasshoppers, and make their chirping by rubbing their wings together. The females have long egg-laying tubes, as you will see if you can catch a mother cricket in the kitchen. She lays her eggs behind the oven or near the fireplace, where they will hatch all the year round in the warmth.

Grasshoppers and crickets do not chirp to please us, they are calling to each other. Therefore they must be able to hear. Where do you expect to find their ears? I am sure you will never guess.

Look under the wing of the small grasshopper on the first ring of his abdomen, the one behind his hind leg. There a little above his breathing holes, you will see a very small hole. This has a thin skin over it, and it is his ear. The great grasshopper has his ear in a still more curious place, on his front leg below his knee.

I expect you will know the Field-cricket, for though it is very timid, and seldom comes out in the day, yet if you find out where it lives, by its chirp, and poke a blade of grass down the cracks of the earth, it is sure to seize it, and you can draw it out. Many country children get them in this way. A Field-cricket is rather larger than the House-cricket; his body is more yellow, and his chirp much more shrill. He is very useful in the garden,

GREAT GREEN GRASSHOPPER'S LEG.
e. Ear.

for he feeds on insects as well as plants, sitting outside his hole at night to catch them. But by day he is always in the ground, where the young ones remain all the winter till they get their wings.

I wonder if you have ever found a Mole-cricket? There are plenty in England in sandy ground, especially in damp fields, and on the banks of canals and rivers. But they do not live in all parts of the country, and they are very shy. only coming out at night. They make a strange croaking cry, and by it you may know that there are some in your neighborhood. Then you must look along the river-bank, or in a sandy and damp part of

1. Great Green Grasshopper – Female with Egg Laying Tube.
2. Small Green Grasshopper.   3. Field Cricket.
4. Long-Winged Grasshoppers.   5. Wingless Female Grasshopper.

the garden, and if you can see ridges of earth thrown up, most likely the Mole-cricket will be working underneath.

He is a very curious insect, about half an inch long with a small head and long feelers, a very broad thorax, and thick flat front legs, ending in large feet like a mole, with sharp black claws. With these he digs his way through the earth, just as the mole does, and his body is covered with soft hairs, brown above, and yellow beneath, to keep off the damp earth. He

MOLE-CRICKET FLYING AND AT REST.

does great mischief if he gets into a garden, for he tunnels along, eating the roots and stems of the plants. The mother Mole-cricket has no egg-laying tube, for she does not want it underground. She lays about 200 eggs in a chamber at the end of the run, and the young Mole-crickets live there for two or three years before they get their wings. If you can find a nest, and get a few of the young ones, you may see their curious shape.

There are two other straight-winged insects which you

know quite well. One is the Earwig, of which some silly people are afraid, though it does no harm to anyone. Its pincers are used to fold its long hind wings under its short wing-cases, and the only mischief it does is to eat our flowers. The mother earwig is very affectionate. She carries away her eggs if they are disturbed, and watches over her little ones till they are full-grown.

The other straight-winged insect is the Cockroach, which people call "black beetle." It is not a beetle, for it does not grow out of a grub, and it is not black but brown. The young are like the old ones, only smaller and without wings. The mother cockroach never has any wings. She carries her eggs in a curious way at the end of her body in a case like a purse, and hides it behind the oven, or under the boards, just before the eggs are hatched. These cases are brown, horny, and shaped something like a bean. Inside there are about sixteen eggs, neatly arranged in two rows like peas in a pod. Cockroaches are very disagreeable and destructive insects. They eat everything they can get, and have a very repulsive smell.

Try to find the different kinds of grasshopper and cricket, both full grown and before they have their wings. Examine the wings of an earwig. Find the egg-cases of the cockroach.

LESSON XII.
ANTS AND THEIR HONEY-COWS.

ANTS are the most intelligent of all insects. We learnt a little about the home of the Hill-ant in Book I., to which you can look back for drawings of the male, female, and worker ants with their grubs and cocoons.

Now we will look at some other ants, and learn about their

ways. There are two very common kinds to be found in most gardens. One is red and the other black. They both build their homes underground, by clearing out the earth with their jaws and feet, and so making galleries and chambers. There is generally a little rise in the ground, where they are at work, making a dome above the nest, but it is not so conspicuous as the hill of the Hill-ant. If you dig a deep hole on one side of a nest you will open the chambers and see the grubs inside them, and, if you do not make it too big, the busy ants will soon put it right again.

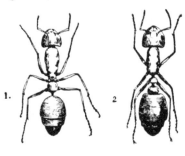

1. BLACK ANT WITH ONE KNOB IN THE WAIST.
2. RED AND WITH TWO KNOBS.

Then you will take a few cocoons, and put them in a little earth under a glass so as to see the young ants come out. But do not take the grubs, unless you take some grown-up ants with them, for they cannot feed themselves.

If you get a black and a red ant you will know them apart, not only by their colour, but because the black ant has one round knob in the thin part joining her hind body to her fore body, while the red ant has two knobs. By this we know that the red ant has a sting, and the black ant has none. All English ants which have two knobs to their abdomen can sting; but those with only one knob cannot (with one rare exception). These which have no sting attack their enemy with their strong jaws, and squirt out a strong acid over them.

There is a little yellow ant which lives in our houses and eats our food. She has two knobs, and stings quite sharply. I once cut open a cake which had been some days in the cupboard and found the middle full of these ants. They swarmed on my hand and made it tingle with their stings. This ant generally makes her home behind the fireplace.

If you put your ants under a glass, and give them a piece of nut or bread to eat, you may see them use their outer jaws to scrape the surface, and their tiny tongue to lick off the juice or oil, while they pass the food to the inner jaws, just as the bees and wasps did. You may also see them pause to stroke their body with their front legs. Look closely at these and you will see a small spur on a joint a little way up the leg. This spur has more than fifty fine teeth on it, and there are some coarse teeth on the leg itself. These are the ant's brush and comb. She scrapes herself with them, and then draws them through her outer jaws, or mandibles, to clean them.

She has very small eyes, and always uses her antennæ to find out anything she wants to know. These stand out in front of her curious flat head, and are very mysterious instruments. When ants want to talk to one another they touch their antennæ, and in some strange way they can tell each other where to go and what to do.

The Garden-ants live much more underground than the Hill-ants, but you may often see them sunning themselves in the garden, or cutting off blades of grass with their mandibles to line their nests, or tearing a spider or fly to pieces. They often seem to run hither and thither as if they did not know what they were doing, but if you watch you will find that each one has an object. Some are carrying things into the nest, others are climbing the stalks of the flowers to sip their honey. As these honey-laden ants go home, if they meet with an ant which has been doing other work and is hungry, the well-fed ant will squeeze honey out of her throat to feed her friend. For it seems to be a rule among ants that each one helps the other.

And now you must watch day by day till you see a much more wonderful thing. You will remember that we saw in the first lesson little plant-lice called Aphides sucking juice out of the stalks of plants. But we did not notice that they have two little horns at the end of their bodies. As they suck and suck they become too full, and the sweet juice often oozes out of these horns. You may see it standing in tiny drops on their tips.

This juice is just what the ant loves, and you may be fortunate enough to see the garden-ant take it, because she brings

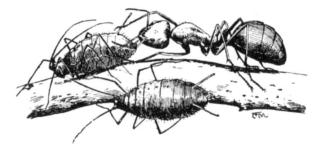

ANT TICKLING PLANT-LICE FOR HONEY.

the aphides and puts them on daisies near her nest. She goes up behind the aphis and strokes its sides with her antennæ, so that it gives out a drop of honey from its horns.

She has another herd of these honey-cows safely hidden underground where you cannot see them. She carries them down into her galleries, and puts them on the roots of plants. There she takes care of them, just as she does of her own grubs, and keeps their eggs and young ones through the winter, ready for the next spring. In our climate ants sleep through the winter, but in warmer countries they remain awake and store up food.

When you are digging into the nest of a Garden-ant look very carefully at the roots you dig up, and you will most likely see some plant-lice on them. If you put them carefully back they will be none the worse, and the little ant will not have lost her honey-cows.

There is a small yellow ant called the Meadow-ant, which lives in great numbers on heaths and meadows, and has no sting. She keeps nearly all her honey-cows underground, putting them on the roots of the grass. Sometimes when you are ploughing up a field you may cut through one of these nests. If you do, stop a minute and watch the ants. Their first care will be for the ant-grubs and cocoons. But as soon as these are carried down you will see them fetching the little green plant-lice as carefully as if they were their own children.

The Hill-ants do not bring their cows home. They visit them on the plants, and many battles between the ants of two nests begin because one colony has interfered with the other's cows. Then the working ants turn out of both nests and fall upon each other two and two, biting with their mandibles and standing on their hind legs, each trying to squirt formic acid over its enemy. These battles often go on for some days till one party is exhausted.

The battles are fought, and the honey-cows are milked, by the working ants, of which there may be thousands in a large nest. The queen-ants do no work, beyond laying the eggs. There may be two or three queen-ants in a large nest, and they never quarrel like queen-bees. When they are laying eggs in the home they have no wings. But in the summer there will be a number of winged male and female ants growing up in the nest, and some warm day they fly out, and you may see them

rising and falling in the air like gnats. Then they tumble help-
lessly to the ground and crawl about. The males are eaten by
birds or die. None of them go back to the nest. Those of the
females which are not killed have their wings pulled off by the
workers, or pull them off themselves, and they go back to lay
eggs, or join a new nest.

*Find any ants you can. Keep them a little, feeding them
with honey and giving them some earth to build. Keep a few
aphides on a plant to see the honey-drops. Examine an ant's
nest by opening the side; put the aphides and cocoons back
carefully.*

Scientific Names of the Orders of Insects, with Explanation.

("*-ptera*" means *wings*.)

A-PTERA........ *Without wings.* Fleas and Lice.

HEMI-PTERA.... *Half-winged*–that is, wings horning in front, and transparent at the back. Plant-bugs, Aphides, frog-hop-
pers, and Water-boatmen.

DI-PTERA....... *Two-winged.* Flies, Gnats, and Daddy-long-legs.

LEPIDO-PTERA.. *Scale-winged.* The wings covered with fine scales. Butterflies and Moths.

COLEO-PTERA... *Sheath-winged.* The front wings horny, forming wing-
cases. Beetles.

NEURO-PTERA.. *Nerve-winged.* Wings covered with a network of
nerves. Dragon-fly and May-fly.

ORTHO-PTERA.. Straight-winged. Wings folded in straight folds like a
fan. Earwigs, Cockroach, Grasshopper, Locust, and
Cricket.

HYMENO-PTERA. Membrane-winged. Wings of transparent membrane.
Bees, Wasps, Sand-wasps, Saw-flies, and Ants.